SHENANDOAH SECRETS

What secrets lie hidden in Shenandoah National Park's forests and briary tangles? What fascinating all-but-forgotten incidents took place inside its boundaries?

Today, Shenandoah National Park is "a play place for city folk," as one old mountain woman said with derision. But not long ago it was simply another 304 square miles of Virginia country-side—a microcosm of an earlier America.

Industry, agriculture, commerce, military action, political decisions, community and family life—all of these have left their mark here. As time passes, these marks grow fainter. But they still linger, at least in memory, as the secrets of another time.

Shenandoah Secrets

The Story of the Park's Hidden Past

by Carolyn and Jack Reeder

The Potomac Appalachian Trail Club

118 Park Street, SE

Vienna, VA 22180

ISBN 0-915746-41-7

Revised 1998 (Second Printing)

Printed in the United States of America

PATC Book Sales e-mail Address: patcsales@erols.com

PATC Telephone Book Orders: 703/242-0968, Ext. 19

PATC Web Page: http://www.patc.net

Other Books about the Shenandoah National Park by the Authors:

Shenandoah Heritage: The Story of the People Before the Park

Shenandoah Vestiges: What the Mountain People Left Behind

Cover: William A. Brown of Old Rag, Virginia

(Photo: Library of Congress)

Table of Contents

Table of Contents

About This Book

SHENANDOAH SECRETS is divided into three major sections. THROUGH THE GAPS is organized from east to west within each gap, and ALONG THE DRIVE and BESIDE THE TRAILS are organized from north to south.

BESIDE THE TRAILS is intended to provide background information that will enhance your enjoyment of the trail. *It is not a hiking guide.* You will need to take a trail map—and to take full responsibility for your own comfort and safety on the trail.

Throughout the manuscript we have used the preferred government spelling of place names that omits apostrophes, *i.e.*, "Browns Gap." (The resort hotel at Blackrock Springs, however, was known as the Black Rock Springs Hotel, and we have used that spelling.) Names of trails and both natural and man-made features in the area are based on the editions of PATC Maps 9, 10, and 11 available in 1997.

A hiker enjoys the view from Marys Rock, about 1928.

Part I

Through the Gaps

Waterwheel, Lam's Mill

THROUGH THE GAPS

For thousands of years before America's settlers found their way through the gaps in the Blue Ridge, those natural crossings were used by wild animals and Indians. In historic times, explorers, armies, heavily loaded wagons bound for market, cattlemen driving their livestock to mountain pastures, and local people going about their daily business passed through Shenandoah National Park's many gaps.

When we speak of a gap today, we usually mean the "saddle" or low point between two peaks. Historically, though, a gap has meant the entire passage across the mountain, including the hollows on either side of the saddle. Today, major highways cross the Blue Ridge and provide access to the Park through Thornton, Swift Run, and Rockfish gaps.

Transmountain routes have existed there since the 1700s. First as pack horse trails and much later as turnpikes, they carried the east-west traffic of their day. Early commercial interests established inns and blacksmith shops along roads through gaps just as today's business people build motels, fast-food restaurants, and gas stations along our interstates. And small settlements grew up along those early routes just as housing developments seem to be spawned by modern highways.

Forest has reclaimed the once-inhabited land in the gaps, but if we look beyond that green canopy and peel away the years, we can uncover some of the Park's hidden past.

Thornton Gap

One of the first roads to cross the Blue Ridge was built through Thornton Gap. It linked the Shenandoah Valley settlement of Massanutting with Thornton's Mill, near today's town of Sperryville. This road later became part of a toll road Peter Marye built from Culpeper Court House, as the county seat was called, to the Shenandoah Valley. Over the years, other turnpikes, including the New Market-Warrenton Pike, used the same—or nearly the same—route.

Scattered along this route were a handful of businesses catering to travelers. But the enterprises that served the local people were clustered in settlements near the mouth of the gap on both sides of the ridge. As time passed, more homes appeared along the turnpike and along the roads that soon branched off it. The lower end of the Pass Mountain Trail as well as several abandoned trails in the Park follow the routes of those old roads.

East of the mountain, a mill complex met most of the needs of the nearby community in the early nineteenth century. This complex, just inside the Park boundary, contained a sawmill, a

The mill complex in Thornton Gap.

Courtesy James E. Swindler

4

Ruins at the Thornton Gap industrial complex. Above: The up-and-down sawmill. Below: The gristmill. Records show that it ground a barrel of flour per hour.

gristmill, and a blacksmith shop. Later, a legal distillery, often referred to in Park records as a cider mill, was added.

The sawmill, built around 1800 by Jonas Clark, was probably the earliest industry in what is now the Park. The vertical blade of this "up-and-down sawmill" was operated by an arm powered by a water wheel. The log moved along a carriage on geared rollers which fed it into the saw. The blade sawed so slowly that the sawyer did other chores—or slept, if he was working all night. Clark is said to have slept with his foot on the machinery so he would awaken when it was time to set the blade for the next pass.

The mountain people benefited in two ways from the sawmill: the men could earn cash by cutting timber to sell, and homes became more comfortable. Before the mill was built, families were limited to log houses with either dirt or puncheon floors. (For puncheon floors, logs were split in half and laid with the more-or-less flat inner surface facing up.) Milled lumber changed all this. Now houses could be faced with weatherboarding, and they could have partitions and smooth, level floors.

The gristmill in the Thornton Gap complex was a clapboard building three stories high. As in other mills of its day, the millstone and funnel-like hopper that held the grain were at the top of the building, and a chute carried the cornmeal to bins on the floor where it was sifted. On the bottom floor was the "wheel pit," where the gear mechanism operated by the water wheel drove all the machinery.

At first, water for both mills flowed through a race from the Thornton River to the site and was diverted into flumes leading to the two overshot wheels. A "spill" below each wheel returned the water to the river. Later, the gristmill's wheel ran the sawmill machinery, too.

Near the mills was a long shed. There, a blacksmith made and mended farm tools and household implements. He also repaired equipment for passing wagoners. When the distillery was added, it was housed in the same shed and powered by the gristmill's water wheel.

Across the road from the mill complex was an overnight stop for wagoners. The Atkins place, as it was called, had a livery stable and a wagon shed. It was a customary stop for the covered

Above: The Hutchins House, at the hairpin curve on U.S. 211, east of Thornton Gap, was the Hutchins Ordinary of a century earlier. Below: In the nineteenth century, travelers lodged at this house, just inside the Park's east boundary. In the 1930s, it was owned by Herbert Atkins.

This house was built by Frank Skinner in 1775 and was known as Skinner's Bower. Later, it was owned by three generations of the Barbee family and was called simply the Bower House. William Randolph Barbee (1818-1868) was known as one of Virginia's finest sculptors. Herbert Barbee, one of his sons, was also a sculptor. The Confederate Monument in Luray is one of his works.

wagons that carried Shenandoah Valley produce to eastern Virginia and returned with manufactured goods.

By the time the Park was established, the area between its eastern boundary and the foot of the mountain was called "Atkins Town" because so many people of that surname lived in there. About two miles inside the Park boundary was a school. A Dunkard church was a mile or so beyond that.

Beginning about 1830, the Hutchins Ordinary stood on the north side of the hairpin bend known as Turnbridge Curve. Its simple accommodations met "the ordinary needs of the traveler." Both the Hutchins place and the Atkins place were still standing when the Park was established, but by then they were simply private homes.

Hawsburg*, the family home of the Barbees, stood in

---

*Some twentieth century sources refer to the Hawsberry Inn, but the Barbee family records refer only to their home, Hawsburg, which provided lodging to travelers as was the custom in the nineteenth century when inns were few and far between.

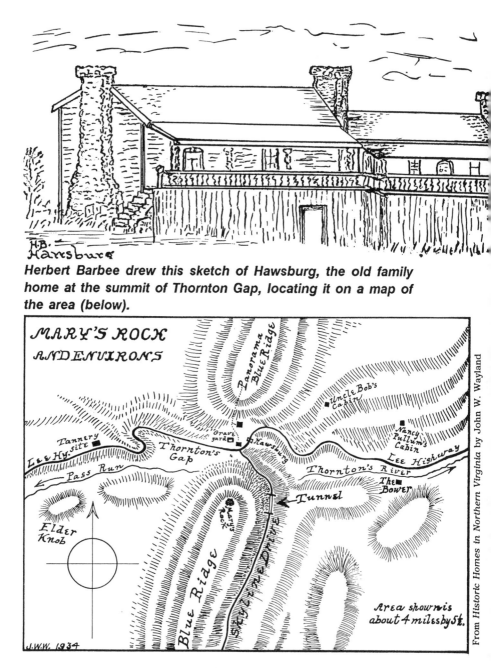

Herbert Barbee drew this sketch of Hawsburg, the old family home at the summit of Thornton Gap, locating it on a map of the area (below).

9

This home, not far from the Bower House, was built over a spring—a style of architecture that enabled the occupants to withstand an Indian attack. Frank (Francis?) Thornton is thought to have built it during the Revolutionary War. Note the hardwood bars in the lower windows.

Thornton Gap just east of the mountain top from around 1785 to 1931. It was an impressive building with a wide veranda. For a time, stages crossing the mountain stopped for the night at Hawsburg. Weary travelers were given a meal and a bed, and the horses were stabled.

Various references mention a tannery and a pottery operating on the Barbee's land in the nineteenth century, and between 1832 and 1858 Hawsburg was a post station. At first, stage coaches carried mail along with passengers, but in 1837 a change in Post Office policy required separate mail stages. These operated on the same principle as the pony express:

> As stage time arrived a fresh four-horse team in full harness was brought out by the roadside. The clattering express arrived at a full trot and stopped with a final lurch of the strap-hung body. The driver tossed his reins down to an attendant while others unhooked the steaming horses. With a quick rattle of chains and swingletrees the fresh four were hooked in and the reins passed to the driver. A crack of the whip and the Warrenton Express was off down the mountain grade to the next post station.

Virginia State Library Picture Collection

The Panorama Restaurant (center) advertised a 75-cent dinner in the mid-1930s. The long driveway led to the Panorama Hotel.

Shenandoah National Park Archives

One of the cottages at Panorama in the 1930s.

11

In the early decades of the twentieth century, travelers found accommodations at Panorama, "a comfortable resort" hotel and cabins near the present entrance station. The hotel was razed, but the restaurant served Park visitors until the early 1960s when the highway cloverleaf claimed its site. (The current Panorama was built at that time.)

West of Panorama, the community that grew up along the road through Thornton Gap was known as "Beahm," after one of the predominant families. For a time, the Beahms had operated a tollgate on the turnpike, collecting the fee and raising the counter-weighted wooden bar to let travelers pass.

Beahm had a school, a post office, and at least two general stores. By the 1930s, one of the stores had a two-pump gas station and a lunchroom beside it where "for 10 cents you could buy a quarter section of a pie about two inches thick." The store and lunchroom stood just a mile and a half west of Panorama, by the owner's comfortable home, a seven-room house with indoor plumb-

Shenandoah National Park Archives

The owner of this house in the Beahm community, Lewis Willis, was a graduate of the University of Virginia. He was one of a small group of mountain residents granted life tenure after his property was condemned for the Park.

ing and electricity generated at the site. One of the most dramatic series of events in the recent history of the area involved this property. The story of the owner's fight to keep his place from being condemned for Shenandoah National Park is a local legend.

Melancthon Cliser believed that under rights granted by the Magna Carta and the U. S. Constitution he was entitled to stay on his land. He fought in every way he could to keep his home and business. As early as 1929, he wrote a letter to the editor of the *Page News and Courier*, denouncing the takeover of private property and trying to rally small landowners to work together to oppose it. More than once Cliser wrote to the Secretary of the Interior. He also wrote to President Roosevelt and even telephoned the White House.

Finally, he simply refused to accept the $4,855 check in payment for his land. Since he hadn't taken the check, Cliser reasoned that the land had not been bought. If it had not been bought, it was still his and he would not leave it. "This is the only home I ever knew and I aim to keep it," he said.

When the Chairman and the Secretary of the Virginia Commission on Conservation and Development came into his store to talk to him about the situation, Cliser told them, "If you want to buy anything, buy it. If you don't, get out." When county officials came to read him an eviction notice, he barricaded himself in the kitchen and refused to listen.

Public opinion was strongly on his side. In fact, it took the threat of contempt of court to get the sympathetic sheriff to carry out the eviction order against Cliser. At last, in October, 1935, the sheriff and four other officers in plain clothes pulled up to one of Cliser's gas pumps in an old car. When Cliser came out to serve them, they promptly snapped handcuffs on him. Resisting to the end, he sang *The Star Spangled Banner* as they led him to the car.

They took him to Luray to talk to the Circuit Court judge who had signed the eviction papers. While the judge tried to explain how the Clisers' home and land could be taken from them, the Civilian Conservation Corps carried the couple's belongings from the house and set them beside the highway. Some of the CCC recruits guarded the Cliser's belongings overnight. But his wife,

13

The Cliser Eviction.

Carrie, had her new fringed window shades ruined, and loom that had belonged to her mother was lost.

A newspaper account quoted a state official who said Cliser wouldn't have been evicted if he'd applied for a permit, as some people in the area had. Then he could have stayed in his home and operated his business on a month-to-month basis.

"But that wasn't the point," said his daughter, Merle Fox. "That wasn't what he wanted. He wanted to stay there and operate his business for good. My father believed in the Constitution," Mrs. Fox continued. "He never got over what happened. He never thought something like that could happen to you in America."

But it did happen. And though the story has become part of the local folklore, each day thousands of people drive unknowingly past the scene of all this drama. Only Carrie Cliser's daylilies, pushing up through the forest floor each spring, hint that the spot was once a homesite.

West of the Cliser place is the site of another nineteenth century industrial complex. By the time the Park took the land, only the gristmill still stood beside Pass Run. But once there was also an up-and-down sawmill and a carding mill.

The carding mill prepared wool for the spinning wheel. It used a system of rollers—two large ones with bristles to comb the fibers and combine them into a thick strand, and smaller ones to move the wool along. The carding mill ran by water power, just as the gristmill and sawmill did.

As manufactured fabrics became readily available, the carding mill shut down. And, as was true east of the ridge, the portable steam-driven sawmill made the up-and-down sawmill obsolete. But in spite of competition from larger operations and from chemical processes, a nearby tannery operated well into the twentieth century.

Elzie Williams' father and grandfather ran the tannery when he was a boy. He described how they extracted the tannin they needed to process hides: "They got the bark off their own trees. They owned a lot of land, enough land so my grandfather gave land to all his seven children. . . . The tanbark was put into a big old iron bowl, a pole was fastened to a horse and a chopper went from the horse into the bowl. The horse went 'round and 'round that bowl and ground the bark for tanning."

Usually, a tannery had at least six four-foot deep vats sunk in the ground. Common sizes were either four-by-six feet or six feet square. Elzie Williams didn't remember how many vats his father's tannery had, but he knew there were three sizes and a separate vat for sheep skins.

Making leather was a long, drawn-out operation. First the tanner prepared the hides farmers brought to him, splitting them for easier handling and soaking them in water to soften them. Next he scraped the skins to clean off fat and tissue from one side and hair and the outer layer of skin from the other. After the tanner washed the clean underskin that resulted, he was ready to start the tanning process.

He began by soaking the cleaned hides in "ooze," a weak infusion of tanbark. He added more bark to the infusion over a period of perhaps several months before he began the actual tanning.

Finally, though, the tanner filled one of his vats with alternating layers of bark and hides and then flooded it with water. During the following months—perhaps as long as a year—acid leaching from the tanbark slowly combined with the gelatin in the hides to toughen and preserve them. The tanner used a hooked pole to turn the soaking hides several times before he dragged the finished leather out of the vat and hauled it to the stream for a thorough washing.

Today, we breathe in the fresh mountain air and enjoy its purity. But when the tannery was operating, the air was rank. The presence of a tannery here was no secret then.

*

At various times between the 1930s and the 1970s, researchers commissioned by the Park recommended preserving or reconstructing some of the historic buildings in Thornton Gap as exhibits. Financial resources were never available, however, and now, time and the elements have made preservation impossible.

Today, a historical marker along US 211 mentions "Hawburg" as the birthplace of Virginia sculptor William Randolph Barbee, but highway construction destroyed the old home long ago. Dense vegetation covers the site of the industrial complex on the east, and the one on the west is most easily located on old maps. The homes that stood along Lee Highway—some dating to before the Civil War—are gone. Only clumps of daffodils, a bit of forsythia, or a length of stone fence hint at two centuries of life and livelihood in Thornton Gap.

Swift Run Gap

One of Virginia's best-known legends tells how Governor Alexander Spotswood led the first organized group of Englishmen across the Blue Ridge at Swift Run Gap and down into the Shenandoah Valley. According to this story, Spotswood later dubbed his companions Knights of the Golden Horseshoe and presented them with little horseshoe-shaped keepsakes. (This was an "in-joke" recalling how their trip had been delayed while the horses were shod after they left the sandy tidewater area.)

Governor Spotswood presented his "knights" with the golden horseshoes on Christmas 1716 in the House of Burgesses, saying, ". . . When the wilderness, which you have discovered and conquered, shall blossom as the rose, as it most assuredly will, these badges may be sought after by the antiquarians of a future age as honored mementos of the first pioneers of their happy and favored country. Let them be religiously preserved, then, I charge you." But in spite of his charge, none of the tiny horseshoes has been found.

The history behind the legend is that Governor Spotswood was convinced that "the boundaries of Virginia must be pushed to the banks of the Mississippi." He also wanted to develop western trade and hoped to find an overland route to the Great Lakes. As soon as he heard that a way through the Blue Ridge had been discovered, he organized an expedition of adventurers to explore the area with him. A party of 63 men (gentlemen, servants, a few Indians, and fourteen "frontier-bred scouts"), 74 horses, and assorted dogs set off. The group's leader, John Fontaine, recorded the details of their 28-day, 438-mile journey.

17

Although two monuments in Swift Run Gap commemorate the Knights of the Golden Horseshoe, some people question whether this was their crossing place. Researchers who followed the route outlined in Fontaine's diary think the expedition actually crossed the Blue Ridge some distance to the north. Milam Gap or Fishers Gap, near Big Meadows, are possibilities.

Wherever it crossed, the expedition created an interest in both westward expansion and land along the Blue Ridge. Investors began buying large tracts of mountain land,* and before many years passed, a trail crossed the mountains at Swift Run Gap. About 1748, the Virginia General Assembly appropriated funds to improve the crossing there, and in 1765 it authorized a road through the gap. This road was called the Spotswood Trail, in honor of the 1716 expedition. Laws authorizing repairs suggest it was heavily used by the 1780s.

The road through Swift Run Gap provided the Shenandoah Valley settlers with access to eastern markets. At first, it was a "rolling road." A farmer would pack half a ton of tobacco into a huge wooden cylinder called a hogshead, fit an axle through the center, hitch mules to it, and roll his harvest across the mountain. This method of transport was well suited to rough and often muddy roads impassable by wagons.

In the early nineteenth century, the road through Swift Run Gap was improved and incorporated into a turnpike. Then wagon trains could carry produce east and return loaded with imported or manufactured goods. Stage coaches could carry mail and passengers across the mountains on the turnpike, too.

The turnpike through Swift Run Gap, like other roads through gaps in the Blue Ridge, played a role in Civil War troop movements. (A late nineteenth-century historian wrote that Lee's army "broke through the mountain passes of the Blue Ridge like a tornado" on the way to Gettysburg.) Thousands of Confederates marched through Swift Run Gap during the war, and cavalry pickets from both sides occupied the gap at various times. Stonewall Jackson's army camped at the mouth of the gap on the west, outside the Park, in the spring of 1862.

---

*The Undying Past of Shenandoah National Park, by Darwin Lambert (Roberts Rinehart, Inc., 1989), gives details of land grants, land owners, and plantation life in the Park and surrounding area.

Lam's Mill, on Swift Run about half a mile from the Park's eastern boundary. According to the oral history of the area, this mill was operated by women during the Civil War.

Near the Park's eastern boundary, Lam's Mill stood along-side the Spotswood Trail. This gristmill operated until the 1930s, but by then a steam engine had replaced its overshot water wheel. The mill had been built a hundred years before and was part of a small industrial complex then. By the early twentieth century, however, the sawmill and tannery were gone.

In the 1920s and '30s, Lam's Mill was a busy place, especially at harvest time. It had two sets of stones and could grind wheat and corn simultaneously, but people still tried to arrive early so the wait wouldn't be too long. (The phrase "wait your turn" originated in the early days of gristmilling.)

Zeda Haney Lam remembered how her brother would throw a sack of shelled corn across their horse's broad back and climb on top of it for the ride to Lam's mill. Zeda loved to go along, but she and the younger children could go only if her brother would hitch "Old John" to the wagon.

The Haneys owned 183 acres where the old Spotswood Trail crossed the mountain in Swift Run Gap. Their home was within sight of the monument to the "Knights of the Golden Horseshoe." Mr. Haney had a general store near where the Park entrance station is today, and when the automobile became commonplace, he added gas pumps. Just across the highway, Ed Mundy had a gas station on land he'd bought from Haney. When business was slow, the two men would chat together. But once people became curious about the new park and the construction of Skyline Drive, there was plenty of business for both of them.

"Skyline Drive split our place in two," Zeda said. "And that was the best land you ever worked on. You could plant anything and it would grow."

Besides corn to grind at Lam's Mill, the Haneys raised green beans to dry for "hay beans." (They spread the beans on sheets on the shed roofs to dry in the sun. Later, Mrs. Haney would cook them for half a day with a hunk of salt pork.) Milam apples grew

Courtesy Zeda Haney Lam

The Haney house at the top of Swift Run Gap early in the twentieth century. The photo shows John and Lula Haney and three of their children.

20

in their orchards. The family dried some of the fruit, made some into apple butter, and stored some over the winter in a ground cellar.

Five cows provided milk and butter. "We'd eat a pound of butter just at breakfast. There were five of us kids, and both our grannies lived with us," Zeda explained. She helped churn butter and make cottage cheese, boiling sour milk to make it curdle and then cooling and straining it. The dry, crumbly curds were stored in a crock, or "stone jar," in the springhouse.

Zeda's childhood memories include playing Halloween pranks, piling onto homemade sleds to coast down the mountainside, picking blackberries for her mother to make into jelly, and gathering chestnuts. "After a windy night we couldn't wait to go out and pick them up! We'd eat some and sell the rest at the store in Elkton." Money they would earn by picking chestnuts bought the Haney children's school books. They walked two miles to the Sunnyside School on the east side of the gap. After seventh grade,

The Swift Run Gap entrance station in the mid-1930s. Notice the Haney house and store and the monuments to the Knights of the Golden Horseshoe.

Shenandoah National Park Archives

21

*Each Sunday,
Lula Haney
recorded the
Sunday attendance
and offering
at the Fern Hill
Church in
Swift Run Gap.*

The congregation at the Fern Hill Church.

Photos courtesy Zeda Haney Lam

Zeda boarded at the CBIS—the Church of the Brethren Industrial School in Greene County.)

One of Zeda's favorite memories was of watching the local stonemasons who built the monument to Governor Spotswood and the Knights of the Golden Horseshoe. The pyramid-shaped memorial in Swift Run Gap was dedicated on September 5, 1921, on the 205th anniversary of the fabled crossing of the Blue Ridge. "It was a big day, and lots of important people came—the Governor, Senators, and everybody," she recalled.

Zeda also remembered the day she saw her first car. She and her brother were churning butter at the springhouse when they heard a strange noise. "Automobile!" her brother shouted. They headed for the highway, calling for the other children to come and see. The five of them sat on the top rail of the fence and waited in great anticipation as the car slowly chugged its way up the mountain on the Spotswood Trail.

As Zeda grew a little older, neighborhood social events became important to her. She loved it when a neighbor phoned and invited the family to a corn shelling or bean stringing, or maybe to a taffy pull or an apple butter boiling. "I caught my first boy friend at an apple boiling," she remembered. "He walked me home, and my mother walked along right behind us."

Before the Fern Hill Church was built across the road from their home, the Haney family walked several miles to the village of Swift Run for Sunday services. But in the 1920s the neighbors raised money to build their own church, and Zeda's mother boarded the carpenters who worked on it. After the church was finished, the Swift Run Gap area where it stood became known locally as Fern Hill instead of just "the top of the mountain." With its store, post office, gas station, and church, Fern Hill was a center of community life.

For many years, Zeda and her husband lived alongside the Spotswood Trail west of the Park. Their place was just a few miles below the sites of her childhood home, her father's store, and the Fern Hill Church—all now graded out of existence. True to her mountain heritage, she planted Milam apple trees in her yard, and every summer she dried some of the green beans from her garden into "hay beans."

*

Between 1832 and 1870, long before Zeda Haney lived at the top of Swift Run Gap, the Mountain Inn provided lodging just inside the western boundary of today's Park. The Mountain Inn was a day's journey from another tavern east of the mountain—just outside the Park. People who could afford the price spent the night in relative luxury both before and after the arduous crossing of the Blue Ridge.

In the last decades of the nineteenth century, woodcutters from Front Royal rode the train to Elkton and walked from there to the village of Swift Run. There they made the inn—known by then as Shipp Tavern—their headquarters. They felled hickory trees in what is now the Park, sawed the wood into 28-inch blocks, and split it into smaller pieces that artisans would later shape into buggy spokes.

The old brick hotel was still the property of a member of the Shipp family when the state bought the land for the Park. The building stood vacant for a time, but in 1940 fire gutted it. Today, faint foundation outlines and a few bricks nearly hidden by underbrush are all that remain.

The people who lived and worked in Swift Run Gap are gone, and few remnants of their homes and businesses can be found today. Though US 33 is called the Spotswood Trail, it doesn't follow the original route over the mountain, and for most of us, Swift Run Gap is simply a Park entrance station now.

Shipp Tavern, earlier known as the Mountain Inn. Its bricks were made in a field 500 yards away.

Rockfish Gap

Far beneath Skyline Drive in Rockfish Gap lies an engineering marvel—the Blue Ridge Tunnel. In 1850, Irish workers with hand drills, picks, and black powder began drilling through the mountain. Following the design of French engineer, Claude Crozet, they progressed through the mountain at the rate of two feet a day.

The project was a joint venture relying on both public funds and private enterprise. The railroad company was to lay the track on both sides of the mountain while the state did the stretch that included the tunnel. Groups of workers drilled from both ends toward the middle, and when they met, they were only half an inch off true center! This feat resolved years of speculation—and wagers—about the possibility of such precise planning.

Plagued by construction problems, strikes, a cholera epidemic, and financial difficulties, the builders took took eight years to complete the 1,273-foot long, brick-lined tunnel. But the railroad company, eager to reap the profits of a transmountain route, hadn't waited for the state to finish it. After the company completed its stretches of track on both sides of the mountain, it built a temporary track through Rockfish Gap. Workers laying track had to contend with stubborn rock and build trestles across six deep ravines. But only seven months elapsed between the start of the project and the first train.

Rockfish Gap entrance in the late 1930s.

Shenandoah National Park Archives

Grades were steep and curves were sharp on this temporary track. There was "barely room for an engine for an ordinary train to stand on the summit before the road slopes off, descending both toward the east and west."

Three special engines with six closely-spaced 42-inch diameter wheels were built for this track. These engines could pull either four fully loaded freight cars or a baggage car and two passenger cars. Each passenger run used "a man at the brake on every platform who never leaves his post." Safety regulations limited the speed to 7.5 miles per hour on the ascent and no more than four miles per hour on the descent.

The railroad used the temporary track at Rockfish Gap from 1854 until Crozet's tunnel was opened about four years later. This tunnel linked the Valley with eastern Virginia for nearly a century before it was replaced by one with greater vertical clearance for larger locomotives. This newer Blue Ridge Tunnel has carried the railroad under the southern end of Skyline Drive since 1943.

Above ground, traffic crosses the Blue Ridge on I-64 and US 250. These are the last in a series of roads that have passed through Rockfish Gap since sometime in the second half of the eighteenth century. The originial "rolling road" was gradually improved, and around 1808 it was incorporated into a turnpike running from Staunton to the James River.

The turnpike was "made by cutting a depth of three or four feet into the side of the mountain and throwing the earth so as to produce a level." In the 1830s, a stage coach passenger described the Rockfish Gap section: "In some places, to the inexperienced, it has an awfully dangerous appearance, running up the side of a steep mountain and having no parapet walls." What a contrast to today's mountain crossing!

Between the end of Skyline Drive and the beginning of the Blue Ridge Parkway, Rockfish Gap now sports a modern highway interchange and an island of commercial development. Few people know of the abandoned tunnel with its brick-sealed entrances lying far below. But Claude Crozet's masterpiece, now a National Historic Civil Engineering Landmark, is the largest and best preserved artifact in the Park. It's the least accessible, too.

Part II

Along the Drive

Skyline Drive shortly before it was paved.

ALONG THE DRIVE

As we cruise along Skyline Drive enjoying the Blue Ridge in its budding spring greenery, its full summer canopy, its bright fall foliage—or its stark ridges through winter's bare branches—we give little thought to the road itself. And we take for granted our easy access to the trailheads along its length.

Before Skyline Drive was built, however, the picturesque peaks and hollows we now enjoy were almost inaccessible. After the arduous trip from Luray, guests at Skyland hiked and rode horseback in the area around the rustic resort. Further south, vacationers once arrived at the Black Rock Springs Hotel by way of Grottoes and then explored the nearby mountains. But it took Skyline Drive to open the Blue Ridge to the day visitor.

Construction of the Drive began in 1931. Drought relief funds paid the workers—local men whose farms were suffering from the effects of the worst dry spell in a century. Congress had appropriated money for a road from President Hoover's fishing camp on the Rapidan River to Skyland and from there to Thornton Gap. The immediate aims were greater security for the President and work for the local people. But authorizing the road led to the fulfillment of a goal set in 1924: the construction of a Skyline Drive that would be the crown jewel of the proposed park.

By the time the roadwork actually began, plans were underway to continue the Drive south to Swift Run Gap. And by the end of the Hoover administration, an extension north from Thornton Gap to Front Royal had been approved.

Because condemnation proceedings to acquire acreage for the Park were proving time consuming, the state bought land for the Drive right-of-way. This required hundreds of separate negotiations, and work progressed in whatever areas had been purchased. Sometimes there were problems: one contractor had to

29

*The Park's first tourists drove along the new Skyline Drive when
the section between Thornton and Hawksbill gaps was opened
briefly before it was paved.*

improve an old wagon road leading up to the ridge in order to get
his rock crusher and other equipment to the construction site.
(That old road is today's Crusher Ridge Trail.)

Building the Drive was a monumental task. First, the route
had to be surveyed and flagged. Then workmen cleared the right-
of-way and grubbed out tree stumps. Next they excavated hundreds
of thousands of cubic yards of earth and rock to prepare the
roadbed. Finally, they laid corrugated metal pipe and vitrified tile
for drainage, poured asphalt, and built rock walls by the roadside.
The job required 134 pieces of major equipment and eleven black-
smiths to keep them all in good repair.

Almost two-thirds of the 161 construction workers were
local men. (Many mountain families stayed in the Park until they
were relocated in the late 1930s.*) The 25 cents an hour they
earned helped offset the loss of livelihood caused both by nature

---

*Our earlier book, *Shenandoah Heritage: The Story of the People Before the Park*, gives
details of mountain life during this transition period.

and by government decree. Besides the drought, nature contributed a blight that wiped out the chestnut trees that had yielded three cash crops: nuts, bark, and wood. Virginia, in turn, imposed restrictions on grazing, woodcutting, and hunting in the Park. The men welcomed the chance to work on the new road.

Even before the Drive was completed, its central section was opened as far as Hawksbill. On the first Sunday people were allowed to drive on the rough-graded surface, the line of cars waiting at the entrance in Thornton Gap extended out of sight. Such a wait is not uncommon on autumn weekends now, but this was 1932! Thirty thousand people traveled between Thornton Gap and Hawksbill before that stretch of road was closed for paving six weeks later.

President Franklin D. Roosevelt was impressed when he was driven up the road from Hoover Camp and along the newly graded Drive to Thornton Gap. To further the project, he immediately designated the first six of the Civilian Conservation Corps camps in or near the Park to provide manpower for beautifying the right-of-way and otherwise assisting the road builders. Roosevelt also favored extending the new road south to the Smokies. His influence eased the completion of Skyline Drive south of Swift Run Gap as well as the construction of the Blue Ridge Parkway.

During the transition years before all the people had moved out of the Park, a ranger offered a mountain man a ride.

"I don't care if I do," the man replied.

This was a local idiom of acceptance, but the ranger didn't know that.

"If you don't care, you can go ahead and walk!" he said, leaving a bewildered mountaineer staring after him as he drove off.

Finally, in September of 1934, the central section of Skyline Drive was officially opened. (By the end of the weekend, the service station operator at Panorama said he was "down to his last three

The Front Royal entrance in the early 1930s.

STOP
PAY 50¢
FEE HERE
DROP IN HOPPER NICKLES
DIMES AND QUARTERS.
THIS MACHINE
MAKES NO CHANGE

DROP
50¢ HERE

The Front Royal entrance in 1956.

gallons of gas." He had counted 4,600 cars turning onto the Drive.) The Front Royal section opened in the fall of 1936, the southern section in late summer of 1939.

Completing the Drive cost about $47,000 a mile, and the rock walls at overlooks and along some slopes cost about a dollar a running foot. It was money well spent. Not until 1983 was a major overhaul of the Drive—and replacement of the original walls and footings—undertaken. This time, the estimated cost was over $326,000 a mile, and summer traffic delays were common. But the continuing enjoyment of the Park and its priceless beauty made it worth both the cost and the inconvenience.

In 1997, Skyline Drive was placed on the National Register of Historic Places. Among the guests at the ceremony were some of the Civilian Conservation Corps veterans who had helped with the road building project more than half a century before.

The Old Simpson Place

Not far from the Front Royal entrance station, you pass the site of Mountain View, a home once owned by a prominent family that played an important role in local history. U.S. Congressman Jared G. Williams gave Mountain View to his daughter Mary and her husband, Samuel Simpson, when they married in 1820.

In the years that followed, Samuel Simpson became a pillar of the community. He served as a justice of the peace, as sheriff, and as surveyor for Warren County. He also established a private school that attracted students from neighboring counties.

When the Civil War broke out, Mary and Samuel Simpson's three sons fought for Virginia. Samuel Jefferson Simpson was the only one who survived to return to Mountain View. Textbooks don't mention a Captain Simpson of the 7th Virginia Cavalry, but he has his place in local history.

During the Shenandoah Valley Campaign, Stonewall Jackson plotted a surprise attack on the Union army occupying Front Royal. In preparation, Jackson sent General Turner Ashby to cut the telegraph lines at Buckton Station, west of town. It was Captain Simpson, with his intimate knowledge of the area, who guided Ashby and his men through the "Fork" section of Warren County. This mission helped assure a Confederate victory in the Battle of Front Royal.

The Simpson family sold Mountain View in 1888. But when the Virginia State Commission of Conservation and Development bought it in 1933, people still called it "The Old Simpson Place." They couldn't forget a local hero.

Belmont

If Marcus Buck had been told that a century after his death hundreds of thousands of people would cross his land each year, he probably wouldn't have believed it. But within a mile of the Park's northern entrance, Skyline Drive goes through Buck's former property. It passes within shouting distance of the place where his impressive home once stood.

In the first half of the nineteenth century, Buck bought nearly 2,000 acres of land on the Blue Ridge. He later sold more than half of it, but he kept the part of the tract that overlooked Front Royal. From that mountainside with its "deep washes, acres of stone, brush, small trees, and weeds" he developed the productive estate he called Belmont. From all accounts, it deserved the name that meant "beautiful mountain."

In its heyday, Belmont had an eight-room house with separate kitchen and office buildings, numerous tenant houses, a distillery and wine cellar, a propagating house that kept several workers busy shipping off cuttings, 75 acres of grapes, and six thousand fruit trees—mostly apple and peach.

Buck built a frame guard around each tree in his orchards as protection from the cattle that grazed there. And every spring he whitewashed these guards. His trees flourished, but viewed from Front Royal, the orchards looked like giant cemeteries!

A knowledgeable and apparently self-taught horticulturist, Buck raised fruit trees from both seeds and "slips," traveling far and wide in search of new varieties. His vineyard, the largest in the South, shipped table grapes to market by rail and also provided grapes for his winery. But when the Civil War began, Buck was forced to farm on a smaller scale. He wasn't able to hire labor and had only five slaves, three of them women.

Belmont.

Throughout the war all Buck's resources—livestock, produce, and fodder—were "drawn upon" by both armies. He also provided food for people in Front Royal who were suffering from the ravages of war. Besides these large-scale demands on his supplies, Buck fed any hungry soldiers who straggled by. He took no payment because he "couldn't bear the thought of charging hungry men for food." He wrote in his diary: "The cry for bread and meat comes up to me from all quarters. How long will I be able to re-

Wine cellar at Belmont.

spond favorably to it? . . . I have given away my grain, fodder, hay and straw until I am nearly out. Not one farmer or family in five has a particle."

Because of wartime disruption of transportation, Buck couldn't ship his fruit to market. So he did what people always did under those circumstances: he made it into brandy. This must have been a successful venture, because it was shortly after the war ended that he built the distillery and a new wine cellar. This "cellar" was actually a three-story building with the first floor holding only 1,000-gallon hogsheads!

When Stonewall Jackson heard two of his officers discussing the merits of French wines in camp one evening, he called for a bottle of wine to be brought from his supply wagons. After the men had debated its origin, he told them it was made by his friend in the Shenandoah Valley. His friend was Marcus Buck.

In the late 1860s, Buck had ten or twelve hands working in his orchards and vineyards. He won prizes with his brandy and fruits, and he shipped wine and brandy to Alexandria, Philadelphia, and Baltimore as well as to more distant cities.

Then, in 1875, Marcus Buck went bankrupt. After he had borrowed heavily to expand his vineyards, wine prices fell drastically. Virginia's first major commercial vintner was ruined, and so were his cousin, Thomas Ashby, and his brother, William Buck, who had co-signed notes for over $100,000. His brother wrote, "I at once transferred to his creditors all the property I owned, real and personal, and stand today divested of everything except my honor. . . ."

The following year, Thomas Ashby accused Marcus Buck of forgery and misrepresenting the state of his affairs. Both public opinion and the court found him innocent, but William Buck sided with Ashby. The resulting rift between the two branches of the Buck family lasted for years.

37

It had taken more than a quarter century of ceaseless effort to turn a mountain wilderness into a productive showplace. And then Marcus Buck had to watch helplessly as Belmont was sold at auction for a fraction of its value.

Belmont, however, still prospered. The new owner used it as a summer place, but his partner lived on the property and managed the business operations. The wine cellars were enlarged, a 5,000-gallon cistern was added, and the orchards and vineyards continued to flourish. A 20-horsepower engine was brought in to grind fruit and grain for the distillery. The vineyards were enlarged. Production quadrupled.

But as time went on, it gradually became apparent that the new Belmont Winery couldn't compete with cheaper California wines sent east by rail. Although Belmont's table grapes continued to be shipped to Washington for some years, the vineyards were no longer profitable.

In the twentieth century, Belmont changed hands several times and the property began to decline. Finally, in 1933, Belmont was bought for parkland. The once-productive land reverted to wilderness, and vandals broke the windows in the white brick mansion that had been considered one of the finest homes in Warren county. When the Park Service razed Belmont in the 1940s to prevent the possibility of a lawsuit resulting from injury to a trespasser, an angry—and partisan—local historian wrote: "That Yankee government, which had tried in vain to destroy Belmont in the martial 1860s, had succeeded in the 1940s when the stout old building was dynamited into its own vast cellars."

Who would have thought that the Park's gentle northern slopes had been the scene of such prodigious agricultural development and commercial enterprise or such human tragedy?

Dickey Ridge

The eastern slope of Dickey Ridge saw action in a battle near the town of Overall (then known as Milford) in September 1864. From the ridge top, a citizen forced to flee the area watched Confederate cavalry form its battle line and saw Union horsemen on a hill a mile away. That afternoon this witness looked down "on men riding, charging, and firing their carbines and pistols." Later, he watched the artillery clash below: "After dark, the passage of the shells through the air could be followed by the streaks of fire that were thrown off . . . and every report could be heard long after the flash from the cannon's mouth."

Today, the view from Dickey Ridge is peaceful, and we come here seeking recreation instead of refuge.

A.T. Crossing at Compton Gap

The 2,000-mile Maine-to-Georgia footpath known as the Appalachian Trail first crosses Skyline Drive at Compton Gap.

Originally, the Trail followed the crest of the mountains. It was built in the 1920s by hardy groups of volunteers from the Potomac Appalachian Trail Club (PATC). They left Washington, D.C., after getting off work at one o'clock Saturday and spent most of the afternoon traveling to the mountains. This left only a few hours to work on the trail before making camp. But they put in a hard day's work on Sunday before starting the long, slow trek back to the city. (One of the early trail builders described the roads they traveled as "a few blocks of pavement in the towns and graded mud in between." He told how after the spring rains, many a farmer kept a team of horses tied to his mailbox, ready to help motorists who mired down. The charge was one dollar.)

Finally, after months of labor, the Appalachian Trail was built and blazed through the Blue Ridge. But then came plans for Skyline Drive, and its route pre-empted much of the newly completed

---

"Remote for detachment, narrow for chosen company, winding for leisure, lonely for contemplation, the Trail leads not merely north and south but upward to the body, mind, and soul of man."

— Harold Allen, PATC (1877-1939)

Trail. Fortunately, the government agreed to rebuild the Trail using CCC labor. But though the young men of the Civilian Conservation Corp built most of the Appalachian Trail in the Park, the spiritual descendants of the original trail builders maintain it. Nearly seventy volunteer overseers from the PATC trim the weeds and brush, restore dry-set retaining walls, and work to prevent or repair erosion damage on the footpath.

Almost 100 miles of the *AT*, as it is affectionately called, lie in Shenandoah National Park. You'll note other crossings of the wide, white-blazed trail as you continue along Skyline Drive. Each is marked by a concrete post giving the mileage to the next crossing or trail junction.

Potomac Appala-chian Trail Club members cleared and blazed the original AT.

Howard S. Olmsted, PATC Archives

Gravel Springs Gap

A "bark road" from Harris Hollow on the east crossed the Blue Ridge at Gravel Springs Gap and led to the tannery at Browntown. You can trace its route on Park maps where the two segments are known as the Harris Hollow Trail and the Browntown Trail.

For two weeks or so each spring, bark could easily be peeled from chestnut, chestnut oak, and hemlock trees. This bark was in great demand because of its high tannic acid content, and local tanneries purchased all that the mountain people could supply for use in curing leather.

Generations of mountain men, sometimes aided by wives and children, cut bark. They felled the trees and then girdled the trunks at intervals, slashing the bark in between and peeling it off with a metal tool called a spudder. "You'd skin you a piece till it broke off and then skin you another. It came off in strips," explained a former mountain man. The bark was stacked to dry and later it was either picked up by tannery wagons or delivered to the tannery. Traces of bark roads can still be found throughout the Park.

A second mountain industry in the Gravel Springs Gap area was making moonshine. "Gravelly Spring was a good place to run off a dubblin'," remembered a woman who once lived not far away. The constantly flowing spring and the abundant apple crops grown nearby made this remote area ideal for distilling brandy.

A load of bark ready for the tannery.

Courtesy Irene Eppard

Beahms Gap

Another road crossed the Blue Ridge at Beahms Gap in the early days. Farmers in the hollows to the east used it to transport produce across the mountain to the railroad station in Kimball. Orchard workers carefully packed apples in barrels for export and loaded two wagons half full. At the top of the mountain, the barrels were combined into one load for the downhill part of the trip, and the empty wagon was driven back to the orchard.

Today, the route they took is used only by hikers. It's known as the Hull School Trail on the east and as the Kemp Hollow Trail (abandoned) on the west.

As you travel along Skyline Drive, watch for the signs that name the gaps and see how often you'll find a trail crossing there. Just as water seeks the lowest level, so does the transmountain traveler.

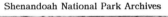
Shenandoah National Park Archives

Mrs. Henry Jewell (Carrie) and her children at their home near Beahms Gap.

Marys Rock

Long ago, people called the mountain that flanks Thornton Gap the Great Pass Mountain, but that name is seldom heard today. Park visitors now speak of Marys Rock—using the name given to the mountain's boulder-strewn summit.

Many legends tell us how Marys Rock was named. In one, Francis Thornton, who owned much of the adjoining land, rode up the Great Pass Mountain with his bride, Mary Savage. From the boulder pile at the summit, Thornton showed Mary his expanse of land and presented it to her. According to this story, the mountain was called Mary's Rock because Mary Thornton was the first woman of European origin to climb it. (Historian Jean Stephenson wrote that after Francis Thornton died, the land in the gap and on the mountain was given to Mary Thornton as dower —property allowed to a widow during her lifetime—and the area was known for years as Madam Thornton's Quarter.) In one variation of this story, Thornton took his daughter Mary to the mountain top to survey his land and she fell in love with the view. In another, Mary Thornton climbed to the summit and returned carrying two bear cubs.

In a different story, Mary was mountain girl who climbed to the mountain's rocky summit to watch for the return of her faithless lover. As she kept her vigil there she was blown over the cliff by a gale and fell to her death.

Two different explanations of the name still circulate in nearby Rappahannock County, but both agree that the peak was named after Thornton's daughter. One version tells us Mary Thornton jumped to her death from the summit because she was in love with two men and couldn't decide between them. In the other, Mary was "crazy." She became lost when she was wandering alone on the mountain, fell off the rocks, and was killed.

Perhaps, though, "Mary" was actually "Marye," and the rock outcrop was named for Peter Marye, builder of an early turnpike through Thornton Gap. This theory is rather prosaic compared to the various legends involving young women named Mary, but it's a compelling one.

Whatever the origin of its name, Marys Rock has been a landmark on the skyline and a hikers' destination for generations. At one time, a spring near the mountain top was a favorite place for the local young men to propose to their sweethearts. If a girl accepted an invitation to go up to the spring on Marys Rock, it was understood that she would accept the proposal. If she didn't want to marry her suitor, she'd decline the invitation and he'd be spared the embarrassment of rejection.

That spring no longer flows. Some people think the blasting of the tunnel through the mountain permanently altered the water table. Perhaps the water that sometimes drips over the tunnel's entrance—or is captured there as an ice sculpture—once bubbled to the surface and provided the setting for a romantic tradition.

Construction of the tunnel below Marys Rock

The Pinnacle Area

During the late 1930s and early '40s, there was a ski slope across Skyline Drive from the Pinnacle Picnic Ground. Sometimes as many as fifty people from Washington, Richmond, Baltimore, and Roanoke came to ski there on snowy weekends. But when the U.S. entered World War II, gasoline rationing kept people close to home, and the Park was used for military training rather than recreation. Park employees no longer kept the bowl-shaped ski slope cleared, and it soon became overgrown with pines. It was never reclaimed.

Just south of the ski area was the site of the first cabin built by the Potomac Appalachian Trail Club for trail workers and hikers. Volunteers built it in 1930 with money donated by Dr. Roy L. Sexton and another club member. (Dr. Sexton had strong ties to the Blue Ridge. He was a frequent guest at Skyland and often traveled into the hollows to bring medical care to the mountain people.)

Groups of club members and their guests enjoyed the Sexton Cabin for several years before the government requested

Shenandoah National Park Archives

Downhill skiers in the Park in 1940.

Above: Bob Sours' home at the head of Jewell Hollow, near the Pinnacle area. Below: Pinnacle Picnic Area was once known as Sexton Knoll Picnic Ground.

that it be removed, fearing contamination of the water supply for the picnic ground and the nearby CCC Camp.

Civilian Conservation Camp No. 10 was located where the Pinnacle Ranger Station stands today (near milepost 37). Beginning in 1933, it housed young men recruited to protect and develop the nation's natural resources in one of President Roosevelt's New Deal programs (see p. 78ff). During World War II, the government converted the camp to quarters for conscientious objectors, and it was known as Civilian Public Service Camp No. 45.

The Pinnacle Picnic Ground was first called Sexton Knoll Picnic Ground. But its name was soon changed to "Pinnacle" in keeping with the government's policy of not commemorating living people. The log pavilion in the center of the picnic ground was built by the CCC, and hidden among the graffiti of present-day vandals are the carved initials of CCC boys who proudly "signed" their work.

For generations now, Park visitors have enjoyed the picnic ground these young recruits built in the 1930s. But that's about all that has remained the same over the years. The Price Lands, as the once-cleared area near Pinnacle was called, are heavily forested now. And today, it is cross-country skiers who are drawn to the Park on snowy weekends.

Stony Man Mountain

The noble profile of Stony Man is easily recognized from Skyline Drive. Today, the mountain is best known for its nature trail, but copper deposits were once its major attraction. Attempts at mining were made by the colonists, and in the 1850s the Miner's Lode Copper Company sank a shaft 60 feet into the north face of the mountain. Although some ore was smelted and carried down a narrow trail by mules, the company's venture was never profitable.

In the mid-1880s, George Freeman Pollock, son of a major stockholder in the copper company, climbed Stony Man and immediately recognized the area's potential as a resort. Partly as a result of his vision, Stony Man Mountain and the other peaks and hollows of the Blue Ridge have been preserved as Shenandoah National Park.

Skyland

Skyland, with its comfortable rooms and pleasant dining hall, began in the late nineteenth century as Stony Man Camp. In 1894, guests slept in tents furnished with cots, chairs, washstands, and pitchers. A "canvas bathing room" and a dining hall that seated about twenty completed the accommodations. Guests paid $9.50 a week for "room" and board. Within three years, a larger dining room and some rustic log cabins increased the camp's capacity to 75 guests, and it was renamed Skyland.

Until Skyline Drive was built, the only way to reach Skyland was to go to Luray and follow a poor road for six miles to the foot of Stony Man Mountain. From there, vacationers could ride up the mountain on rented horses, hire a driver to take them up in his horse-drawn buckboard, or walk four strenuous miles. In the summer of 1898, a Skyland guest left Washington, D.C., on the 10:45 train one night and arrived at six o'clock the next morning. This was considered "pretty good time."

Skyland in the early days.

Shenandoah National Park Archives

George Pollock, Skyland's flamboyant founder and proprietor, woke his guests with an early morning bugle call. During the day he led hikes—and later horseback rides—on trails he had constructed. In the evening he provided entertainment ranging from his own famous rattlesnake show to minstrels and musicians from the Shenandoah Valley.

One of the beer steins from George Pollock's collection. Mary Morris, of Front Royal, cherishes this stein Pollock presented to her mother at a party. And she remembers her mother's amazement at the extent of Pollock's collection: "He had walls and walls of them— everywhere you looked, there were beer steins. He had them from thimble-size on up."

Families and singles, many from the Washington and Baltimore areas, vacationed at Skyland year after year. Some of them rented cabins; others bought lots and built cottages or lodges of their own, giving them names like Fern Cabin, Peter Pan, and Tryst of the Winds. The Park Service has preserved the Pollock's private quarters, Massanutten Lodge, which is located on the road below the dining room. Like many of the original buildings, it is shingled with great slabs of bark.

Above: Skyland guests outside bark-shingled cabin.
Below: The new cabin in Corbin Hollow, financed by Skyland
guests, and the old one it replaced.

George Pollock couldn't have built and operated Skyland without the local people. In the early days, they spent countless weeks clearing the land, digging out the stumps, and hauling away the rocks. Many of them walked for miles over rough trails to spend the day working at Skyland's stables, in its kitchen and dining room, or on its grounds. Besides the forty or fifty regular employees, Pollock often hired carpenters and stonemasons to build or remodel cabins.

The mountain people were always welcome at Skyland, and they often came to watch the evening entertainment. From the fringes of the group around the campfire—or peering through windows and doorways when the program was indoors—they caught glimpses of a different world.

Besides boosting the local economy and enlarging the community's horizons, Skyland directly affected the lives of the mountain people. In 1915, Pollock and his guests held a fair to raise money to build a better cabin for an impoverished Corbin Hollow man. And in the late 1920s they started a school in Nicholson Hollow. Doctors who summered at the resort provided health care for the local people, and guests often brought clothing and food packages for them. (Later, there were complaints that some of the mountain people learned to "beg" as a result of their relationship with Skyland guests.)

*

George Pollock had been running Skyland for almost forty years when he received a newspaper clipping from his Washington friend, Harold Allen, who often visited the resort. The article said that a committee had been named to recommend a location for a new national park in the southern Appalachians. "Why not Skyland?" Allen had penciled in the margin.

That summer, when he arrived at the resort, Allen brought with him the committee's questionnaire. He and another guest helped Pollock fill it in, and Allen hurried off to hand-deliver it to the committee's secretary.

From 1924 on, much of Pollock's prodigious energy was devoted to assuring that his beloved Skyland and the surrounding Blue Ridge would be protected as part of a national park. First, he built new trails and observation towers on Stony Man, Hawksbill,

51

One of Pollock's observation towers.

and two other peaks. Then he offered his resort as a show place where individuals and organizations promoting the Blue Ridge could wine and dine the decision makers. The views from Skyland, the easily accessible White Oak Canyon Falls, and the Limberlost's virgin hemlock forest impressed all who saw them.

Pollock's public relations work succeeded. In late 1924, the Southern Appalachian National Park Committee recommended the Virginia Blue Ridge for the East's first national park.

The bugle no longer blows at Skyland, bonfires no longer provide light for entertainment extravaganzas, and the mountain people are gone. But Pollock's hope of keeping his 6,000 acres out of the hands of the timber cutters and available for public recreation has been fulfilled—and then some.

Addie Nairn Pollock, wife of Skyland's proprietor, did her part to preserve the beauty of the area. In 1929 she bought the choicest of the hemlock trees in the Limberlost Swamp near Skyland to save them from being cut by lumbermen.

Crescent Rock

A 1933 newspaper article with a Luray dateline announced the possibility of putting a bounty on rattlesnakes in Shenandoah National Park. "The largest rattlesnake den in Virginia, according to old residents, is located . . . near 'Crescent Rock,' one of the wonder spots of the Blue Ridge." The article went on to claim that as many as fifty rattlesnakes a day had been killed there and that the area was also infested with the "deadly copperhead."

But Crescent Rock was more noted as a spot for outdoor religious services in the Park's early days than for its snake population. An extra-large parking area was built at the overlook in recognition of its use for revivals and Easter sunrise services.

There was a more secular use of the area, as well. Former Park Superintendent Taylor Hoskins told how during the early days of the Park four young local men used to meet and play musical instruments at the Crescent Rock Overlook. When people gathered to listen, the musicians offered to sell them moonshine from a supply they had hidden in the rocks.

In those days, people called Crescent Rock "Sours' Rock," after an area family. (Misunderstandings of the mountain dialect led to reports that it had been known as "Sow's Rock" or "Sarah's Rock.") A young woman who had been jilted is said to have thrown herself off the rock, and a moonshiner claimed to have escaped the revenuers by leaping from it. Now, however, tourists park at the overlook, and Crescent Rock is simply another of the Park's magnificent viewpoints. The days of snake infestation, religious fervor, music, and moonshine are past.

Hawksbill Gap

Today, Hawksbill Gap is known mainly as a trailhead parking area for hikers planning to climb Hawksbill Mountain or to set off along the Appalachian Trail or down Cedar Run. But in the mid-1930s, the Madison County newspaper's column on local communities included Hawksbill Gap news submitted by Delon Taylor.

Delon and Hester Taylor raised eight children at their home in the gap, and Delon taught them all to read and write. Their home was within sight of Skyline Drive, but it's lost to forest now. The Taylor family cemetery is just east of the Drive, though the original field stones and the metal markers have not survived the years. The burials there reflect some of the tragedies of mountain life—three of Delon and Hester's grandsons who died in infancy, and a married daughter who died as a result of a stove fire.

Hawksbill Gap trailhead in the 1930s.

54

A funeral at the Taylor Cemetery in Hawksbill Gap.

Bernie and Annie Taylor with their children.

Bernie Taylor, one of Delon and Hester's sons, lived with his family "just a short walk" from the house in the gap where he grew up. He and his wife, Annie, were the parents of the three little boys buried in the family cemetery.

According to Mozelle Cowden Brown, a social worker in the Park area before the mountain people were relocated, Bernie Taylor was one of the finest men you would meet anywhere. She told of the dilemma he faced when the doctor said his anemic child should have meat.

"I can't get meat because I can't hunt in the Park, and I can't raise hogs or chickens because the wild animals get them, so I don't know what I'm going to do," he said.

"Well," Miss Cowden replied, "if my child was sick and I lived among wild animals, I'd get some meat."

Later, she went to the ranger and asked him to leave Bernie alone if he saw him hunting. He replied that he'd be away for the next week. Miss Cowden returned and told Bernie this.

"Well," he mused, "I've always tried to follow the rules."

Her answer to this was, "The people that make the rules don't always know what things are like for you people. I told you before, I'd get me some meat. And I'd get it while the ranger is away."

Bernie thought for a minute and then replied, "I think I could manage that."

The child recovered.

Spitler Knoll

"Spitler's Ranch" included about 320 acres west of Skyline Drive and north of the Spitler Knoll Overlook. Influenced by a trip to the West, Bernard Spitler, who owned the land, dressed like a cowboy and ordered his cattle from Chicago instead of buying them locally.

Each spring, Spitler drove his cattle a dozen miles or so from his Page Valley farm to his mountain property. There they grazed on "the best blue grass in the country" until late fall when the cattle buyers came. After weighing the animals on Spitler's scale, the buyers drove them down the mountain to the railroad in Stanley and shipped them to market. Because western livestock matured faster than eastern varieties, Spitler saved himself the expense and effort of feeding them over the winter.

When the Park took over his grazing lands, Bernard Spitler lost more than the most profitable part of his farming operation. For more than twenty years he had spent his weekends and vacations with family and friends in the spacious house on his property. Although he lived within sight of the new park, Bernard Spitler never visited it. He didn't want to see his grazing land and garden return to forest or his house reduced to rubble.

The house on Bernard Spitler's grazing lands. During the winter, Spitler's tenants, the Jim Woodward family, lived here.

Shenandoah National Park Archives

Bernard Spitler, Jr., never saw his father's "ranch," but he likes to explore the old site. Sometimes he thinks about how, if things had been different, the land would now belong to him. He says that for many years the concrete foundation of the house was visible just off the blue-blazed trail leading to Rock Spring Cabin. Thickets of roses his father had planted bloomed there, too. But in the 1970s the foundation was removed and the roses were uprooted, apparently in an effort to return the area to its natural state.

Bernard still has the mechanism for his father's cattle scale stored in his barn. And one of his prized possessions is a picture of the vacation house his father so enjoyed. "Everybody knows how hard it was for the mountain people to give up their homes for the Park," he says, looking at it sadly. "But nobody ever thinks about the Valley farmers who lost their grazing land."

Fishers Gap

One of the transmountain routes that linked the Shenandoah Valley with the Piedmont crossed the Blue Ridge at Fishers Gap. A turnpike was built there in the mid-nineteenth century (see pp. 135-136), but some sources mention an earlier road. The Park's yellow-blazed road through Fishers Gap follows the old turnpike route.

In November 1862, Stonewall Jackson's army crossed the Blue Ridge through Fishers Gap on the way to Fredericksburg. Jackson camped in the gap with his staff, and he's believed to have stood on Franklin Cliffs, a short distance north, watching his army struggle up the mountain. The following July, General Jubal Early crossed here after the Battle of Gettysburg. He was en route to Culpeper, where General Lee was reconcentrating his army following the retreat.

Before the Park, Shenandoah Valley farmers used the road through Fishers Gap to drive their herds to mountain grazing lands each spring and back home again in the fall. They called it the Red Gate Road because of a prominent red gate at the top of the ridge. That section of the old transmountain road is still known as the Red Gate Road even though it's now barred by a black and white Park Service gate.

Big Meadows

Big Meadows is probably the best known area of Shenandoah National Park—a welcome expanse of open land in the midst of forested mountains. Old maps show that the meadow was once much larger. It extended from Fishers Gap on the north to a mile south of Bootens Gap, and from Tanners Ridge on the east nearly as far west as Hoover Camp. Today, the Park keeps a fraction of the original area open by mowing.

From earliest times, Big Meadows was considered prime grazing land. Records of Shenandoah Valley town meetings show interest in using it for summer pasture as early as 1732. When Big Meadows became parkland two centuries later, it belonged to a Shenandoah Valley family that had used it as summer cattle range since about 1870. Mountain families lived on the land as tenants, looking after the cattle and extending the meadow by cutting timber for their own use. This mutually beneficial relationship between the Valley landowners and their mountain tenants has been compared to the feudal system.

From the windows of the Big Meadows Visitor Center, you often can see deer browsing in the meadow. And, depending on the season, you might see berry pickers, kite fliers, or cross-country skiers. But in 1933 you would have seen what amounted to a small city inhabited by as many as 200 young men! Then, Big Meadows was the site of Camp Fechner, one of the first CCC Camps.

The Shenandoah National Park dedication ceremony at Big Meadows in July 1936.

Virginia State Library and Archives

President Roosevelt visited the camp a few months after it was established and ate the noon meal with the enrollees "from an aluminum mess-kit out of doors." Three years later, he came to Big Meadows again, this time for the Park dedication.

It was a well-planned event. Officials made Skyline Drive one-way south before the ceremony and one-way north afterward, and tank wagons along the Drive sold gas and oil. Forty-five state troopers kept traffic moving and protected the president.

The ceremony was broadcast over coast-to-coast radio hook-ups—still a novelty in those days. The official program was opened with music by the U. S. Marine Band, and President Roosevelt formally received Shenandoah into the national parks system as a gift of Virginia. He dedicated it to all Americans "for the recreation and for the re-creation which we find here."

Hezekiah Lam, shown here with one of his daughters, sat beside Franklin D. Roosevelt at the Park dedication ceremony, representing the local people. Later, when asked how he felt about sitting next to the President, he replied, "Well, it ain't helped me none and it ain't hurt me none."

Big Meadows was known as "one of the most ideal sites in America for the sport of gliding." The 1934 National Glider Meet was held on the meadow.

Photos Shenandoah National Park Archives

The first camper arrived five minutes after Big Meadows Campground officially opened. (A "ghost forest" of blight-killed chestnut trees extended from near today's Visitor Center to the campground.)

Milam Gap

According to tradition, Joseph Milam, who once lived in this gap, had an apple tree that bore such fine fruit people came for miles to make cuttings. They grafted these "slips" onto their own root stock so they, too, could grow these superior apples. This was the origin of the Milam apple that was highly regarded by the mountain people because it kept well through the winter and made excellent brandy.

You may notice that the Appalachian Trail crosses Skyline Drive in Milam Gap. The *AT* route here is the remains of an old road—once a major route from New Market to Madison Court House, today's town of Madison. Confederate General A.P. Hill's division reportedly took this road east in November 1862 while the rest of Jackson's army was crossing at nearby Fishers Gap.

Years later, Jim Colvin was a tenant on the grazing land in Milam Gap, then a part of Big Meadows. When President Hoover built his fishing camp on the Rapidan River two miles east, Mrs. Hoover bought hand-loomed rugs from Colvin's wife. A few years later, Eleanor Roosevelt also bought the mountain woman's rugs.

There's no sign today that a famous general or two presidents' wives ever passed through Milam Gap. But remnants of a homesite and the apple trees that bloom along the Drive each May are enduring evidence that ordinary people once lived here.

Bootens Gap

Just north of Bootens Gap, you'll cross the famous Fairfax Line. It was plotted in 1746 by a team of surveyors to mark the boundary of the 2.5 million acres inherited by Lord Fairfax.

Fairfax's land was bounded on three sides by the Chesapeake Bay and the Potomac and Rappahannock rivers. A line between the sources of the two rivers was the fourth boundary, and the surveyors' job was to map it. They started near Bootens Gap, at the the Conway River, which a survey ten years before had mistaken for the source of the Rappahannock. That earlier error nearly doubled the size of Fairfax's true holdings and included land that had been granted to others. Fairfax's agents and those of James

Above: The Thomas House in Milam Gap about 1935.
Below: When Hezekiah and Mary Lam were married, he was past 60 and she was 42 years younger. They are shown here outside their home in Bootens Gap with three of their six children.

Barbour (who actually owned the land) sold or granted many of the same tracts. Nearly a century passed before the courts settled all the resulting controversies.

Then came the Civil War and Reconstruction. Much property was lost in tax sales, causing new confusion about land ownership; sometimes speculators bought land without the knowledge of the people who lived on it. Such transactions set the stage for heartbreak later. In the 1930s, many people whose families had farmed the land for generations received no compensation for property condemned for the Park. (About thirty so-called "squatters" were granted equity by court action and were paid, but tenants received nothing.)

Many writers think the mountain people's suspicion of outsiders began with the years and years of land disputes that date back to 1746 and the erroneously drawn Fairfax Line.

South River Picnic Area

The picnic ground at South River is on a gently sloping knoll. It blends into the surroundings so nicely that it seems to have always been there. But not only were the tables, grills, and other amenities provided by the Park Service, the knoll itself reportedly was created by the CCC boys, who brought truckload after truckload of fill dirt into the area to cover the rocky ground.

When the Park was established, Luther Dean operated one of the area's many stave mills near where picnickers relax today. The workmen lived at the site, and Matilda Breeden, a local woman, cooked for them. Her cabin was near the old South River Shelter, which is now a trail maintenance hut.

Earlier in our history, coopers made barrels one at a time, hand-riving the staves, shaping them with a drawknife, and then assembling them. But with the advent of power machinery, staves were mass produced at mills.

At the beginning of the twentieth century, commercial development of refrigeration and cold storage encouraged local apple growers to enlarge their orchards. The orchardists, who shipped their fruit to market in barrels, bought staves by the wagonload and hired coopers to assemble them. Throughout the Park area, stave mills sprouted up to meet the demand.

At the stave mill, a steam engine operated the machinery, and the escape steam was used to steam the lengths or "bolts" of wood. These bolts were cut while still hot. Every stroke of the "cutter" sliced off a stave. Over a thousand could be cut in an hour—enough to make more than seven dozen apple barrels.

"Bolts" of wood for the stave mill.

Workers stacked and dried the staves before running them through the "jointer," a machine with two circular blades that beveled the edges so the finished barrels would be tight. (Sometimes the children of families living near the mills collected the shaved-off strips of wood for kindling.) Another machine, the "crozer," then shaped the ends of the staves so the cooper could fit them neatly against the barrel heads.

If you picnic at South River, you won't see any signs of the industry that operated there well into the 1930s. And you'll hear children's shouts and bits of adult conversation instead of the hiss of steam and the clatter of machinery. You might see an occasional sawmill in rural areas near the Park, but now that apples are shipped in wooden bins, stave mills are things of the past.

One of the many stave mills originally within the Park's boundaries.

Vernon Foltz, a local man, built this "unauthorized" service station on Skyline Drive near South River.

Dean Mountain

Although the houses were a quarter mile or so apart, the area from Dean Mountain to Swift Run Gap was a close-knit community. "On that mountain, people were good to one another," remembered one local resident. "They lived like neighbors."

But in May 1925, a murder shocked the Dean Mountain community and families for miles around. The events of that spring night were memorialized by a ballad:

> *My name is Gruver Meadows, my name I'll never deny.*
> *I done a cruel murder, and in prison I will die.*
> *Now listen my good people, just listen to what I say.*
> *I killed my wife and Stanton Dean on the 11th day of May. . . .**

Gruver Meadows seemed an unlikely murderer. He owned over a thousand acres of valuable timberland on Dean Mountain and operated a stave and sawmill there. He was considered a good businessman and was a member of the Fern Hill United Brethren Church. A local newspaper account described him as a "man of good appearance and pleasant countenance." It went on to say:

> If in a crowd, he would doubtless be the last man to be picked out as the perpetrator of such an attrocious crime as that with which he is charged and is said to have confessed. . . . The only explanation for the tragedy is, that when Meadows committed it he was possessed of a murderous brain storm.

Gruver Meadow's wife, Serena, was "a woman of excellent reputation," according to the news report. And Stanton Dean, who worked for Meadows' logging operation and boarded with the family, was "a hard working exemplary young man in the opinion of all who knew him." He was well loved as the singing teacher at the Fern Hill Church in Swift Run Gap. No one who knew the two victims believed there was any reason for Gruver Meadows to suspect an adulterous relationship. (Meadows had explained to his older

---

*Words by Mildred Blori and Nina Monger; music and record by Gooby Jenkin.

children that he'd killed their mother and Stanton Dean because he could tell by signs that they were "doing ugly.")

On the night of May 11, Gruver Meadows went into the small bedroom off the kitchen where Stanton Dean was sleeping and shot him in the head. Then he went upstairs and shot Serena, who had run into the hall outside their bedroom.

> *My anger still a-raging, I caught her by the hair.*
> *I beat her and I threw her, I did no longer care.*
> *But to her I would not listen, she pleaded in despair.*
> *And then with smoking pistol, I shot and killed her there. . . .*

Meadows told the five younger children to stay in their room while he took his twelve-year-old son and set off toward a neighbor's house to ask for a ride to Harrisonburg. There, he turned himself in to the Rockingham County authorities. (As soon as they discovered that the Meadows home was just across the line in Greene County, the case was transferred to that jurisdiction.)

Word of the murder spread quickly, and neighbors flocked to the house, sure there was some mistake. They looked through the window and saw where Serena Meadow's blood had trickled through the upstairs floor boards to form a pool near the kitchen stove. There was no mistake. Then the authorities arrived, after a five-mile walk from the Spotswood Trail in Swift Run Gap—the closest road easily passable by automobile.

> *I went to town next morning, and I told what I had done.*
> *I surrendered to the sheriff, and I laid down my gun.*
> *They put me in the jail house, I tried to play insane.*
> *The people all against me, my intentions was in vain. . . .*

No one doubted Gruver Meadows' guilt—he was convicted of murder and sentenced to prison, where he died nearly half a century later. His motherless children were cared for at Greene County's Church of the Brethren Industrial School, which held his land in trust to provide for their support.

The Dean family folklore explains Gruver Meadows' motive: he planned his double murder so he would appear to be a wronged husband. He thought he would be acquitted for his "crime of passion" and be free to marry the young women he had fallen in love with.

The ballad that tells of this murder may no longer be sung, but the story is still remembered. It has been handed down in the families of those who lived in the mountains and were shaken by the events of the spring of 1925.

Hensley Hollow Overlook

In April 1862, two companies of Stonewall Jackson's men marched into Hensley Hollow. There they broke up a camp of disgruntled local men who were defying the Confederate government. One account states that three or four hundred Unionists from Greene and Rockingham Counties had fortified themselves in the hollow. Another says Rockingham County militiamen, angered by passage of the new Conscription Act that made their term of service the duration of the war, holed up there.

Whatever the men's motivation, Jackson ordered an end to their insubordination. An elderly woman who lived near the fugitives' hideout reported that the general had "sent a foot company and a critter company to ramshag the Blue Ridge and capture them."

During Civil War, deserters hid out in the mountains of Greene County. Because of the Union sentiment of many locals, they were seldom pursued.

Hightop

As you drive south from Swift Run Gap, Hightop looms ahead of you. It seems aptly named. But in the late 1930s and early '40s, efforts were made to change its name to Mt. George and to rename the peak northeast of it Mt. Spotswood.

The diarist John Fontaine, who recorded the 1716 crossing of the Blue Ridge by Governor Alexander Spotswood's party, wrote:

"We called the highest mountain Mt. George and the one we crossed over Mt. Spotswood." And eight years later, another member of the party wrote that the Governor "cut his Majesty's name in a rock" on the highest peak at the crossing, naming it Mt. George. The writer added that the group called the peak next in height Mt. Alexander, after Spotswood. All this was accompanied by the drinking of a great many toasts to English royalty and the firing of volleys in their honor.

A Charlottesville man lobbied tirelessly for restoration of these historic names. Although the Virginia Historical Society supported him, his request was denied. Authorities refused to change the names of the two peaks because they couldn't be positively indentified as the ones referred to in the diary. Government officials pointed out that local historians have claimed every breach in the 15 miles between Fishers Gap and Swift Run Gap as Spotswood's crossing point.

The casual Park visitor will identify by name only the distinctive Marys Rock, Stony Man, and Old Rag. And it matters little to the Appalachian Trail hiker climbing Hightop that the mountain is known by a descriptive name rather than a historical one. But it took three years of correspondence to settle the issue.

Nearly half a century before Spotswood's expedition "christened" Mt. George, John Lederer, had explored the Blue Ridge. Lederer's journal account suggests that he may have traveled west through Swift Run Gap and climbed Hightop in 1669. But his expedition, made up of a few Indian guides rather than a large contingent of gentlemen, lacked the kind of fanfare that creates legends. No one has suggested renaming Hightop "Mount Lederer," and it's unlikely anyone will.

The Simmons Gap School.

Simmons Gap

In the 1920s and 30s, Simmons Gap was a thriving community with an Episcopal mission as well as a general store and post office. Besides its church and school, the mission provided a recreation hall and sold donated clothing at low prices because most of the mountain people were too proud to accept charity. The church sponsored an adult Bible class, a junior Bible class, a primary class, and the Simmons Gap Community Singing School.

One autumn day, the teacher at the Simmons Gap Mission School noticed an unpleasant smell and traced it to one of her students. She sent a note home asking the mother to give her child a bath. When nothing changed, the teacher sent another note. Finally, she told the child to ask her mother to bathe her. The next day the little girl came back with a message: her mother said she'd been sewn into her clothes for the winter and wouldn't be let out till June!

Before the mission was established in 1900, one Simmons Gap man sent his children to a school across the mountain. Their instruction came to an abrupt end, however, when a child fell off a log footbridge and drowned.

When Frederick William Neve, an Archdeacon of the Episcopal Church, showed interest in helping the community, a school was the people's highest priority. One resident offered a newly built cabin for the school house, and a family agreed to board the teacher in a small cabin just yards from their own. Some of the cabin's window panes were gone, and "the woodwork had drawn away from each side of the stone chimney, leaving crevices through which the wind could blow without hindrance." But the young teacher moved in and set to work.

Soon a churchman donated money to build a school on his grazing land in Simmons Gap. This was the first of the "schoolhouse-chapels" built in the Blue Ridge under the sponsorship of Archdeacon Neve.

Neve held services there whenever he could. In the early 1900s, however, the round trip from his home just north of Charlottesville to Simmons Gap took three days. So young David Lewis volunteered to spend the summer preaching to the people. He took the train to Island Ford, west of the mountains, and walked the ten miles to the Simmons Gap Mission carrying his satchel.

At first the people grumbled, wondering why Neve had sent them a boy instead of coming himself. One man told seventeen-year-old David that he ought to go back home to his "Mar." But soon his preaching attracted such crowds that the schoolhouse-chapel was filled. People even stood outside and listened through the windows.

A visiting preacher was not so well received as Archdeacon Neve or David Lewis, however. The congregation sat patiently as he droned on and on at an evening service, and this encouraged him to talk even longer. Finally one of the men in the back of the church got up and walked to the door. He peered outside and then called, "She's a-riz!" The whole congregation rushed out the door to find their way home by the light of the newly-risen moon.

Three decades later, the Simmons Gap Mission, now a thriving enterprise, held a "Homecoming Day." The Junior Auxilliary put on a play, the church school gave Bible recitations, a student presented a prize paper on George Washington, and the 4-H girls showed the dresses they had made from clothing bureau donations and remnants. Samples of school work were proudly displayed, as were the jellies, preserves, and canned goods that had won prizes at the county fair. And everyone enjoyed the lunch the girls prepared under the supervision of the County Demonstration Agent: fried chicken, salads, bread, cakes, pies, and cookies.

The mission played an important part in life at Simmons Gap, but as in most rural communities, the general store was a center of activity. Here the men gathered to play marbles. "They had a cement ring made down in the road," remembered Raymond E. Morris. "Sometimes over 100 people [were] there. Most times five on a side was partners, but you know everybody mostly got into it before the game was over." It was a fight over a marbles game —in which "some people got knocked in the head with rocks"—that resulted in Park officials closing the store in 1936.

Above: PATC hikers and community members on the porch of the Simmons Gap store and post office, about 1928. The bicycle wheel is a calibrating device for measuring trail mileage. Below: The recreation hall at the Simmons Gap mission.

Besides the marbles games at the store, people played "town ball" on a diamond near the mission and held square dances accompanied by banjo and fiddle players in the recreation hall. That handsome stone building is all that remains of the Simmons Gap Community. You can see it just east of the Drive, on the old road through the gap, where it is used as a ranger station.

Hiking north from Simmons Gap on the Appalachian Trail, about 1930.

Loft Mountain

Loft Mountain is opposite the Wayside at mile 79.5, in one of the Park's developed areas, but the best view of it is from the Loft Mountain Overlook about five miles north.

Thousands of vacationers follow the self-guiding Deadening Trail or the Appalachian Trail along Loft Mountain's slopes each year, but once it was so inaccessible it was known as "Lost Mountain." Miles from the nearest gap, Lost Mountain had no road linking it to Piedmont or Shenandoah Valley towns. A family's only contact with the outside world was the Valley farmer whose cattle they cared for.

Then early in the twentieth century, the scene was set for change. Archdeacon Neve (page 71) saw Lost Mountain silhouetted against the dawn sky and vowed that "the sun of righteousness" should also rise there. He went to talk to the people on the mountain, and they asked him to build them a school. This was the beginning of the Lost Mountain Mission.

Even before the schoolhouse-chapel was built, however, David Lewis, who was spending the summer in missionary service at Simmons Gap, walked the five miles to Lost Mountain to preach. His spellbound congregation sat on rocks and logs and refused to leave even when it began to rain. The people later told Neve that they had decided to give up swearing and live a better life because of the young man's sermons.

By the 1930s, all Lost Mountain's school-age children attended the mission school, and the average attendance at Sunday School was thirty—more than half the mountain's population. But again, the scene was set for change. The mission worker wrote:

> The Shenandoah National Park, so long a name to us all, is becoming a reality. The lands are being bought up now in our section. The Lost Mountain . . . waiting and massive, is right on the path of this Park ogre. I am told that when the buying is finished there will be only one family left on that mighty mountain. . . . The mission property is not in the park area. We are left with a complete plant and no people to whom to minister.

No longer isolated and inaccessible, the mountain's name has metamorphized from "Lost" to "Loft," and few people wonder at its origin. Fewer still know—or care—that it was once called Frazier Mountain because so many Fraziers lived there. But the name of the Valley family that owned bluegrass pastureland on Loft Mountain—and on Big Flat Mountain where the campground and picnic area are located—lives on. The Appalachian Trail north of the campground passes through pastureland still known as the Patterson Fields. And the Patterson Ridge Trail follows the route the Pattersons used to drive cattle to their mountain grazing land.

Ray Wood grew up on his grandfather's place in the Pasture Fence Mountain area. He remembered how on Sundays he and his friends sat along Skyline Drive and watched the cars because there was nothing else to do. He said they might see as many as six a day.

Browns Gap

Originally, Browns Gap had two names. People on the east side called it Brown's Gap, after the influential family that owned over 6,000 acres in that area. But on the west, people called it Madison's Gap, after the family that settled on the Valley side. Today, Park maps show Browns Gap Road east of Skyline Drive and Madison Run Road west of the Drive.

One of Virginia's oldest east-west trails ran through the gap. In 1805, Brightberry Brown and William Jarman began building a turnpike across the mountains following this old trail. Brown was responsible for the eastern leg of the road, Jarman for the western. According to legend, when their two crews met at the top of the ridge, a fist fight erupted in a dispute over which group had built the better road.

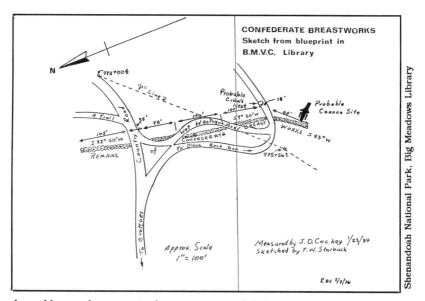

Local legend supports the presence of defenses built during one of the times the Confederates were in the Browns Gap area. Some skeptics, however, suggest that this sketch may simply show the remains of a farmer's stone fence.

During the Civil War, Stonewall Jackson began the most active period of his famous Valley Campaign offensive in Browns Gap. On May 2, 1862, his army left camp near the present town of Elkton, marched south to Port Republic, and then swung eastward through the gap as if heading toward Richmond. But it was a feint. Just west of Charlottesville, Jackson loaded his men on trains and sent them back to the Valley through the Blue Ridge Tunnel at Rockfish Gap. They met and defeated Union forces near McDowell, a town west of Staunton.

After subsequent victories at Front Royal, Winchester, Cross Keys, and Port Republic, Jackson's army returned to Browns Gap and camped there more than a week before heading for Richmond. It was a well-earned rest. In just over five weeks, Jackson had marched his "foot cavalry" more than 400 miles and won five battles. His Shenandoah Valley Campaign had tied up Union forces numbering about three times his own, keeping them from joining the advance on Richmond.

Once, a man who lived where Skyline Drive now crosses Browns Gap walked to town and asked the doctor to come and see his wife, who was unconscious. When the doctor arrived, he found the woman lying motionless on the bed with her eyes closed. But he knew her well—apparently she was somewhat of a hypochondriac—and doubted that she was in a coma. He also knew that she was "quite a dancer."

So the doctor sat down beside the bed and asked the woman's son to play a fiddle tune. Soon the patient's fingers began to move in time to the music. Noticing this, the doctor told the son to play some "good old foot-patting music." It wasn't long before the woman was out of bed and dancing!

Besides its commercial and military value, the road through Browns Gap gave the local people access to the world beyond the mountains. Better medical care was one of the benefits it brought them. In remote areas of the Blue Ridge, it could take several days to get word to the nearest doctor and for him to find his way to the cabin. But the mountain people near Browns Gap just followed the road west to the town of Grottoes to fetch the doctor.

The road through Browns Gap was closed to the public in the late 1930s, much to the dismay of people in nearby Valley towns who still complain about the long detour around the Park to reach Charlottesville. But it's still open to hikers and horseback riders, and with only a little mental effort, you can imagine what it would be like to be a Civil War soldier marching through this famous gap.

In most parts of the Park, the local midwife assisted at childbirths, but in the area near Browns Gap, the doctor from Grottoes often came and delivered babies. Once when he asked a father how many children he had now, the man said, "Well, I don't know. You see, some live here and some live at their grandmother's." But when the doctor asked him how many dogs he had, the man immediately responded, "Fifteen."

Dundo Group Campground

The Civilian Conservation Corps was the first group to camp at Dundo. Imagine Dundo in 1937 with hundred-foot-long barracks instead of tents and a mess hall instead of picnic tables. Visualize administration buildings, officers' quarters, a garage, and a hospital.

CCC recruits at Dundo lived rigorous lives. They woke to a 6 a.m. reveille and scrambled into their blue denim work uniforms for a physical training session. Then they hurried to the mess hall for breakfast—typically stewed prunes, cereal, and large quantities of ham and eggs, coffee, and milk. Before roll call and inspection, they cleaned their barracks and the grounds.

From 7:45 a.m. until 4 p.m., recruits fulfilled the Corps' mandate of performing "useful public work in connection with the conservation and development of the natural resources of the United States." Sometimes they tore out gooseberry and wild current bushes—hosts for the blister rust that was destroying the Park's stately white pines. Other times the recruits built trails and picnic grounds. They were always on call to fight forest fires.

After work, most of the young men spent some time on the sports field before they changed into their dress uniforms for dinner. For the rest of the evening they could attend classes ranging from basic literacy and health to vocational training in tractor operation, mechanics, carpentry, and stonemasonry. If they preferred, they could play pool and table tennis or leave the camp in search of other entertainment until "lights out" at ten.

For their work, the recruits received $30 per month—good wages during the Depression years when so many men couldn't find jobs. The government sent $25 of this home to their families, thus extending the reach of this New Deal program. Five dollars was ample spending money, since housing, meals, and clothing were provided.

Most of the "CCC Boys" thrived on camp life, and many reenlisted when their six-month term was over. But in November 1937, mutiny broke out in five of Shenandoah's CCC camps, and more than 100 recruits were dismissed because they wouldn't work! At one camp, twelve men went on strike, refusing to work on Armistice Day (now Veterans Day). Others refused to work at all.

CCC recruits worked to beautify Skyline Drive.

The CCC was often called upon to help deal with emergencies such as this slide on Skyline Drive.

Newspapers quoted one of the men discharged who told his commander, "Up where I come from no one of my class works with a pick and shovel and I don't intend to start." Reporters heard another say, "Why should I work? My mother is on relief, and she will support me."

In general, however, the CCC Boys worked hard and willingly. They branded the dissidents as "quitters who couldn't take it." Investigation showed that most of them were from Pennsylvania's mining districts and were used to striking when things didn't go their way. They were ill-prepared for the rural environment of the camps and continuously clashed with the work-oriented southern recruits.

Despite occasional difficulties, the CCC continued until Congress abolished it shortly after the U.S. entered World War II. It was one of the most successful and popular New Deal programs and one with positive long-term results as well. The CCC Boys at Dundo and the Park's other camps left a grand legacy of camp-grounds, picnic areas, rustic rock walls, and trails.

Trayfoot Mountain got its name from the huge bear a hunter tracked across its slopes—a bear so large its footprints were "almost as big as a dough-tray."

Via Gap

Like many gaps Skyline Drive crosses, Via Gap bears the name of a family that lived in the area. The Vias moved to the Blue Ridge in the 1700s and bought land along the Moormans River. When the land was condemned for Shenandoah National Park, thirteen tracts were owned by Vias. Two of the tracts belonged to Robert H. Via, and he didn't want to give them up.

Some landowners resisted the condemnation of their land by writing letters of protest, some by posting signs or brandishing weapons, and some by legal action. Robert H. Via chose the latter route. He took his case all the way to the U.S. Supreme Court.

Via questioned "whether Virginia has power to condemn land with the sole purpose of making it a gift to the national government for national park purposes." He argued that if the federal government didn't use the land for a park, he'd have no redress from the state.

By the time the Supreme Court agreed to hear the case, more than a decade had been devoted to promoting and developing the Virginia Blue Ridge as the site of the East's first national park. These years were spent raising money to purchase the land, establishing boundaries, surveying and then appraising the tracts involved, and making plans to relocate displaced families. Skyline Drive was being built, and the CCC had been at work for two years.

When the Supreme Court upheld earlier decisions against Via, the people who had worked so hard for Shenandoah National Park must have felt an enormous sense of relief. The last obstacle to the realization of their dream had been removed. It was November 19, 1935, when the Court ruled on *Via vs. Virginia*. The Park Service, which had delayed some of its planned projects, set to work again, and less than eight months later the president dedicated Shenandoah National Park.

Crimora Lake Overlook

From the Crimora Lake Overlook, you can see two bodies of water far below. Crimora Lake is the smaller one. Once a reservoir for the Crimora Manganese Mine, it lies just outside the Park's western boundary and was formed by damming a mountain stream. The larger, aquamarine "lake" to the left is actually one of several of the mine's water-filled open pits.

Prospectors discovered manganese deposits along the western foot of the Blue Ridge during the early nineteenth century. But the significance of these deposits wasn't recognized until after the 1856 discovery that adding a small amount of manganese during the smelting of iron produced better steel. Realizing that northern furnaces burning anthracite coal were making Virginia's charcoal-fueled iron furnaces obsolete, the mining industry turned its attention toward the manganese deposits.

Crimora Mine was named for a young girl who caught the fancy of one of the mine's first operators. The earliest records show that it was worked in the late 1860s and that most of the ore was exported to England and Belgium.

A prospector's tunnel in the Park.

Crimora Mine.

Later operators, abandoning the original open pits and shallow shafts, drilled deep shafts with side passages at various levels. During the decade beginning in 1882, the mine operated at maximum production. Then early in the twentieth century, hydraulic mining methods were attempted, using water brought from mountain streams by flumes. This was unsuccessful, however, because the water supply was inadequate. The mile-long tunnel driven through the quartzite into the lower part of the manganese deposits—a three-year effort—never fulfilled its promise.

Until World War I, the U.S. imported most of its manganese from Brazil, India, and Russia. But the start of the war provided an economic incentive for domestic production. In 1915 Crimora Lake was created. A pipeline brought the water around the west end of Thorofare Ridge to the steam-powered mill at the mining site. There, clay was washed away from lumps of manganese brought to the mill in cable-drawn cars.

World War II caused the next increase in demand for manganese, and strip mining began in 1943. By the next year, Crimora Mine was the largest single manganese producer in the U.S. But it shut down shortly after the war, once again unable to compete with low-cost imported ore.

The mine that was once world famous for the quality of its ore lies abandoned. Thorofare Mountain's forested slopes screen from view much of the scar mining operations left on the landscape, but you can still see Crimora Lake and one of the water-filled pits.

Jarman Gap

Jarman Gap was first called Woods Gap. Michael Woods (Wood, according to some sources) and his family were the first to cross the Blue Ridge there. They came up from the Shenadoah Valley in 1734, the first known settlers of the mountain lands. Around 1800, Thomas Jarman bought the ridge-top land in the gap, and since then people have called it Jarman's or Jarman Gap.

Three years after Woods settled on the east side of the gap, the county court issued him an order to clear a road "From the Blew Ledge [as the Blue Ridge was then called] down to Ivy Creek." His stretch of road was intended to be part of a route linking the Valley town of Staunton with Richmond. Because it was marked by notches on trees along the way, it became known as Three Notched Road.

During the Revolutionary War, thousands of British and Hessians captured at the Battle of Saratoga were marched to a prison camp near Charlottesville. When the British army approached the city in November 1780, the prisoners were evacuated via the Three Notched Road. A British officer wrote of the trip through Woods Gap:

> You scarcely perceive until you are upon the summit that you are gaining an eminence, much less one that is of such prodigious height, owing to the judicious manner that the inhabitants have made the road, which by its winding renders the ascent extremely easy. After travelling near a mile through a thick wood before you gain the summit of these mountains, when you reach the top, you are suddenly surprised with an unbounded prospect that strikes you with amazement.

84

Later, Virginia's leaders feared that crops from the fertile Shenandoah Valley would be sent north to Maryland and Pennsylvania by way of the Great Wagon Road instead of along poor roads to eastern Virginia. So the state authorized a turnpike to connect Staunton with the James River. It was built around 1826, incorporating the nearby Rockfish Gap Turnpike to cross the Blue Ridge. After that, the road through Jarman Gap began to lose its importance as a transmountain crossing.

In more recent years, Jarman Gap was described as "the center of a corn liquor distilling area." Hikers scouting a route for the proposed Appalachian Trail in the late 1920s were warned away from the area by Valley residents who suggested they would be lucky to return alive. The hikers walked through the area without incident, but they reported feeling they were being watched.

Shenandoah National Park Archives

"Revenuers" discovered this still in the Park and arrested the moonshiners. In 1932, law enforcement officers destroyed 3,504 stills and confiscated 282,562 gallons of whiskey in Virginia.

Originally, Jarman Gap was the Park's southern boundary, and the Blue Ridge Parkway began there. But in 1961, the boundary was changed; now the Park and its Skyline Drive extend to Rockfish Gap, where the Parkway begins. Between the two gaps, much of the Park is only the width of the Drive's right-of-way.

*

For some, Skyline Drive is almost synonymous with Shenandoah National Park. The 105 miles of secnic highway—and the Visitor Centers—are all the Park many tourists see. Though there's much, much more, the Drive and the interpretive signs at its overlooks provide a marvelous introduction to the treasures and pleasures beyond it.

An early view from Skyline Drive showing the Valley shrouded in mist.

Part III

Beside the Trails

Mother and child with pets in Corbin Hollow.

BESIDE THE TRAILS

Many of the Park's trails follow the routes of old turnpikes, wagon roads, logging or bark roads, and paths used by the mountain people. Beside these trails you often see stone fences or rusted strands of barbed wire, chimneys and foundations, or discarded household items such as the ubiquitous washtub. You might see ancient boxwoods and lilac bushes or pass a cemetery with both fieldstone markers and carved memorials.

Much of what happened here, however, left no mark on the land. Historical works have a few references to these events, and some accounts were written during the Park's formative years when interest in the area and its residents was high. But it is the descendants of the mountain people who have kept much of the Park's story alive as family lore.

Knowing what happened beside the trails can add another dimension to your hike, engaging your imagination as well as your senses as you walk in the Park.

The Fox Farm

The interpretive trail across Skyline Drive from the Dickey Ridge Visitor Center takes you to the site of the Fox Farm. Coming into this old homesite, you'll pass the small family cemetery where Lemuel Fox is buried. His was the second generation of Foxes that lived here, and three more were to follow before Virginia purchased the land for Shenandoah National Park.

Lemuel's father, Thomas Fox, settled here as a tenant farmer for Marcus Buck (see p. 34ff). Thomas had a 450-acre farm with 150 acres cleared, and in time he accumulated the $5,000 needed to purchase it from his landlord.

Lemuel grew up in the seven-room log house his father built. Horses, sheep, and cattle grazed in acres of bluegrass pasture, and corn, wheat, rye, and oats grew in the fields. The large garden included a grape arbor—not surprising in view of the nearby Belmont vineyard.

When the Civil War came, Lemuel and two of his brothers fought for the Confederacy. One brother died of typhoid, the other fell in battle at nearby Ashby Gap. Only Lemuel returned to the Fox farm to live with his father and step-mother and their eight young children.

In 1871 Lemuel brought home a wife. Two years later, Thomas Fox died and Lemuel had to support his father's second family as well as his own. He sold timber and tanbark for cash, and the whole family gathered chestnuts to sell. Together, they worked in the orchards, gardens, and grain fields. Maintaining more than 130 productive acres required everyone's help. Often, Lemuel's children were too busy with farm work to walk the 3.5 miles to Harmony Hollow School.

Like many mountain people, Lemuel is buried near where he was born and where he toiled to support a family that would work the land when he was gone. Unlike many others, his grave is not overgrown by brambles or hidden by fallen trees.

When the Park was established, 465 families still lived within its boundaries. Scores of others had already sold their land to the government and moved away. Where were all these people's homes? And where are their ancestors buried? Shenandoah's lush vegetation is part of its attraction, but with every passing year it becomes harder to find the old homesites and graveyards that lie off the beaten track. Some are lost forever.

But thanks to the Park's interpretive program, Fox Farm is no secret, nor is Lemuel Fox's final resting place.

"Sawmill Jim" Clatterbuck and his family lived near the head of Gooney Run.

The A.T. North from Compton Gap

Walking north on the Appalachian Trail from Compton Gap, you'll pass through an area where exploiting forest resources was a way of life. Beginning in the nineteenth century, the mountain people cut chestnut trees and sold the tannin-rich bark to the tannery in nearby Browntown. And in the first third of the twentieth century, much of the tract was heavily lumbered.

You can find the rusting remains of a sawmill by leaving the *AT* at the intersection a few hundred yards from the gap. (Skip this detour in summer because of heavy undergrowth.) Take the grassy road that leads east to the old Indian Run Shelter, now a trail maintenance hut. At the fork, turn left and go downhill toward the spring, the source of Indian Run.

The sawmill artifacts lie not far from the south bank of the stream about 250 feet below the spring. An 1880s vintage steam engine, fueled by bark slabs cut from the logs, provided the power, but it's no longer there. In 1982, the Park gave a group of steam engine buffs permission to remove it. They dragged its rusting hulk for two miles along an old wood-hauling road they had cleared. Retrace your steps to the *AT* when you are through exploring.

At the next *AT* intersection, make a short detour, this time following the Dickey Ridge Trail to the Fort Windham Rocks. This rock formation has been known by that name as long as anyone can remember, but its origin isn't known.

West of Fort Windham Rocks is a spring once known locally as Lehew Spring. When Front Royal was a frontier town, a typhoid epidemic struck the area, and the Lehew family fled into the mountains. They took with them their slaves, some of whom had already fallen ill, and built six or eight log cabins near Fort Windham Rocks. They lived there, drawing water from the nearby spring, while they nursed their slaves back to health.

Return to the *AT* and continue north. Just before the Park boundary, you will come to a viewpoint known as Possums Rest. After you admire the vista, look down and try to imagine the steep hillside below you as the cornfield it was in Alex Pomeroy's day.

In the nineteenth century, Pomeroy owned several hundred acres of land around Possums Rest. One year his piglets began to disappear, one at a time—victims of a marauding bear. After it killed the sow, Pomeroy tracked it to a den in the rocky ledges below Possums Rest and killed it.

For many years, Pomeroy wore a coat made out of the bear-skin, and then he used it for a blanket. "He got right much use out of that old bear," said his granddaughter, Lola Wood, remembering the often-told family story.

The Little Devils Stairs Circuit

One of the Park's most popular hikes is the Little Devils Stairs Circuit. Apple trees, stone fences, remnants of old buildings, and a well-maintained cemetery hint at the area's past. If you stop to read the stones in the cemetery on the Keyser Run Road, you will learn the names of the area's predominant families. And you will

The Gore House, near the top of the Little Devils Stairs canyon, was one of the oldest houses in the Park area. Its last owner was Richard Dwyer.

92

see the toll once taken by infant mortality. Nearby, you can explore the homesite where a prosperous mountain family lived.

Beulah Bolen grew up at the old John Bolen place below the cemetery where an abandoned road intersects the Hull School Trail. The house was lit by carbide gas lamps, and the family had a telephone, too. (The line ran to Kimball Central, west of the mountain, and to the homes of many of their mountain neighbors.) Beulah remembers the wallpaper and the beautiful carved mantel-pieces above the fireplaces in five of the eight rooms.

Frances Bolen Dwyer (left) and her sister, Caroline Bolen Wood-ward. Mrs. Dwyer raised 14 children and two grandchildren in the old Gore House (at left). The counterpane in the back-ground is one she made. She grew the flax, spun it into thread on her spinning wheel, dyed it, and wove it on her loom.

You can see the covered spring beside the road and remnants of the springhouse immediately below it. In Beulah's childhood, the family's Maytag washing machine was in the springhouse along with the trough for cooling crocks of perishables.

"The washer ran on gasoline," Beulah remembers. "You started it just like a lawn mower, and sometimes it took about as long to get it started as it did to do the wash! We heated the water for it in an iron pot over a fire we built just outside the door."

Below the spring stood a large building that had been a distillery in Beulah's grandfather's day, when licensed stillhouses were legal. In Beulah's childhood it was used to store wagons and buggies, and she remembers rolling old spinning wheels along the floor of its loft on rainy days.

West of the spring, along the abandoned road, you can still see part of the foundation of the old barn. Next to it was the hog pen, and then came the corn house. Corn on the cob was dried and stored in its three rooms, and apples and root vegetables were stored in its cellar. The wagon shed was close by. "We sheared the sheep in there, and that's where we kept the apple drier we used one year. It had screens to spread the apple slices on over a wood fire underneath."

Keyser Run Road above the Bolen Cemetery in the early 1930s.

The Bolens also had a meat house at the corner of their yard. They dried and salted most of their meat, canning the rest or preserving it in brine.

For the Bolens, as for all mountain families, storing food for winter was an important concern. A small room at the corner of their back porch had bins for cornmeal and flour. "A couple of barrels lasted all winter," Beaulah remembered. "And we bought a barrel of salt herring at Schwartze's Store and made a barrel of kraut for the winter, too. We kept them in the springhouse."

As a girl, Beulah gathered eggs, milked cows, helped shear sheep, and plucked geese for feather beds. ("If you didn't hold them tight enough, they'd peck you and eat the buttons off your dress!") She also made soap and sometimes helped cut wood with a two-"man" saw. She and her brothers and sisters earned pocket money by selling black walnuts and dried apples. They sliced the apples and spread them out to dry on low shed roofs. "You had to bring them in before the dew fell," she remembered, "but we liked that way better than using the drier Father bought."

Shenandoah National Park Archives

The Bolen Place, built by John Henry Bolen who "was known for three counties" for the product of his legal distillery.

The Bolen children walked to Hull School for the first seven grades. If they wanted to continue their education, they went to high school in Sperryville, the nearest town. It was such a long walk to where they met the school bus that Beulah's older sister Nina boarded in town during the week.

Beulah's parents owned 1,000 acres and four tenant houses. One of the tenants, Hube Baker, came and used their blacksmith shop to shoe their horses. While he was there, he also half-soled the family's shoes and mended things for them. Beulah's father, Bernard Bolen, let Hube cut wood to sell in Sperryville when he needed cash.

All this activity may be hard to imagine as you pause outside the wall that surrounds the Bolen Cemetery or walk among its gravestones to read the dates and epitaphs. Visualizing yesterday's farms in the midst of today's forest isn't easy, but the people who lie here once worked sunny fields not far from where they now rest.

Courtesy Beulah Bolen

Today, the cemetery on the Keyser Run Road is surrounded by forest, but once it stood in the middle of a cornfield. Beulah Bolen remembers how she and the other children would chase each other along the top of the wall.

96

Catch As Catch Can

John Henry Bolen spent the Civil War years evading the conscriptors who combed the area looking for men of draft age. Once the conscriptors came in the daytime when John Henry was in the house, and he had no way to escape. Thinking fast, he sent his wife outside and had her walk toward Pignut Mountain hitting two shingles together. Since the conscriptors thought she was signaling her husband to stay away, they didn't bother to go into the house.

John Henry Bolen

When the conscriptors came on a summer night, John Henry and a friend took refuge in the chimney, one standing on the other's shoulders. Mrs. Bolen slapped the baby playing on the floor near the hearth so its crying would mask any noise they made.

Eventually, though, John Henry Bolen and his friend were caught and taken to an army camp, but they escaped and came home—wearing out their shoes on the way.

Pole Bridge Link and the Keyser Run Road

Many of the Park's trails or roads are named after a geographical feature—a hollow, a mountain, or a creek. But where did they get the name Pole Bridge Link? A glance at the map shows that it links the Keyser Run Road and Piney Branch Trail, but what about the pole bridge? Well, it washed down the Piney River years ago, but its name lives on.

The same cannot be said for the name of Jinney Gray. Martha Gray was a landowner in the area in the mid-nineteenth century, and the road up the mountain was probably named for one of her descendants. One story tells us that it was named for Jinney Gray because the young men from the nearby CCC Camp beat a path to her door. But like so many other stories without a known source, this one is clever but false. The road was named long before the CCC was even thought of.

At any rate, generations of hikers used the Jinney Gray Road, enjoying its gentle grade, before the Park renamed it "Keyser Run Road" in 1980. More than one experienced hiker was momentarily disoriented upon first seeing those unfamiliar words on the concrete signpost! And more than one group of novices with an out-of-date map thought they were lost until someone set them straight.

If you hike on the Pole Bridge Link, you will be in "the region of Andrew Gaunt." In the mid-nineteenth century, Gaunt (rhymes with "ant") owned about 485 acres in the relatively flat area between Pole Bridge Link and the eastern sections of Piney Branch and the Keyser Run Road.

The Gaunt family had an eight-room home and enough cabins for about 25 slaves. They cleared the land and raised wheat, corn, and potatoes, flax to spin into linen, peaches and cherries to dry, and apples—some to dry, some to store in straw-lined pits, some to turn into brandy, and others to sell. Horses, cattle, sheep, and goats grazed on their land, and their hogs foraged for acorns and chestnuts in the woods.

This family's life was more than a frontier existence. The list of items auctioned off after Andrew's death included mahogany and walnut furniture, china, silver, pewter, glassware, and a 36-hour clock. Other items on this list show how busy the distaff side of the family must have been: a loom, spinning wheels, spool racks, yarn winders, flax wheels, counterpanes, china jars used in preparing pickles or sauerkraut, and candle molds.

In the mid-1970s, some of Andrew Gaunt's descendants met to hike through the plateau where he had lived. His great-grandson later wrote of the respect he felt his ancestors' self-sufficiency:

Do we live better? By all material standards of course we
do; but we certainly have lost, as our lives have become
more regimented, circumscribed and protected, a degree of
mastery of our own souls which our forebears enjoyed.

As you walk near the area where Andrew Gaunt's family
and slaves lived and worked, the relative flatness of the land might
suggest that it was once farmed. But the years, the elements, and
the forest long ago removed almost all traces of habitation here.

The A.T. from Rattlesnake Point
South to Range View Cabin

In the early 1930s, the Potomac Appalachian Trail Club (PATC)
began work on a cabin in the northern section of the Park.
Because its location was a wide expanse of cleared land with
sweeping views of the surrounding mountains, Range View Cabin
was an appropriate name.

The land around the cabin was part of a nearly 1,500-acre
tract owned by Dr. J. T. Kelly, who had grazed livestock there
since 1908. Besides sheep and cattle, Dr. Kelly had such a huge
herd of goats that local people called his place the Kelly Goat
Farm. He wanted to develop first-class sod grazing on his virgin
land, and he raised goats because of their voracious eating habits.
They browsed on new shoots and saplings and kept his cleared land
from growing up in brush or forest. Dr. Kelly had developed about
300 acres of sod before he lost his land to the Park.

When the PATC chose the spot for their new cabin, they
didn't know who owned the land, and it didn't matter to them that
the Park would soon take it over. They needed a base camp for
trail workers, and they'd found the ideal location.

Volunteers from the Club did much of the work on the site,
but they hired mountaineer Charlie Sisk to haul the rocks on his
horse-drawn "slide" and to do the stone work. Charlie was an
excellent mason. Some said he'd learned his skill "courtesy of the
Commonwealth of Virginia."

It was widely known that Charlie had served time for killing a man who had bested him during a drunken rocklifting contest. He became something of a local legend. Stories still circulate about how Charlie Sisk, a trusty, would let himself out of jail, go home for a brief visit, and lock himself back in with the guards none the wiser. One story says he whittled a key from a chicken bone he'd saved from his dinner plate.

Charlie himself admitted to only one fault: he "liked to bend the truth a little." Some think he originated many of the stories that made him a legend.

Charlie's reputation as a killer, as well as his masonry skill, served PATC well. Workers on the Range View Cabin were constantly harrassed by a gang of "juvenile delinquents" led by a Page County man. These hooligans cursed and insulted the club members and threw stones at them, shouting that city hikers and campers weren't welcome there. And then, after the workers left, the gang would vandalize the site and steal any materials they could carry off. Appeals to the county sheriff brought no results, so Charlie Sisk put a stop to the problem.

One morning when he and his helper laid out their tools, they set out two shotguns within easy reach. When the hooligans saw those guns, their insults died in their throats. They dropped the rocks they'd been about to throw and slunk away—for good.

When the cabin was being built, there was no Skyline Drive. To reach the site, workers had to leave Lee Highway (U.S. 211) and drive over five miles of dirt road along Piney Branch, fording the stream "innumerable times."

After parking the car at a mountain family's home, the trailmakers faced either a steep, rocky 3-1/2 mile climb up the Piney Ridge Trail or a more gradual five-mile hike along the Piney Branch Trail. Which way would you have chosen if you'd been the one who had to pack in the cabin's cast-iron stove?

The cabin was completed in 1933 and has been used by hikers ever since.* Today's visitors, however, don't have quite the same experiences as those who stayed at Range View in the early years. Before the landowner was forced to abandon his grazing

---

*For information about reserving Range View Cabin (and other trailside cabins in the Park), contact the Potomac Appalachian Trail Club.

land, cattle lay in the spring and "stood outside the door, and the manure became so thick that you could hardly get in and out." (Fencing the spring and cabin quickly took care of this problem.)

A decade later, visitors to Range View Cabin found that their competition was the U.S. Army. An entry to the cabin's log book in 1943 read, "After two wonderful nights are leaving as Army moves in for maneuvers. . . ."

Another visitor wrote: "Regret to note horse manure in immediate vicinity of cabin and spring. Cavalry personnel, evidently responsible. . . ." The following summer, Army dog training units were seen frequently in the cabin area.

Now, forest has reclaimed the surrounding land, and the cabin has lost its "range view." As you approach it on the *AT* or Piney Ridge Trail, it won't be easy to imagine you're walking through some of the 300 acres of prime sod pasture developed by Dr. Kelly—with the help of his goats.

Hull School Trail

The Hull School Trail was once part of a road through Beahms Gap. Farmers in Frazier and North Fork Thornton hollows hauled their produce across the mountain to the railroad town of Kimball on the Beahms Gap Road. If you walk down the Hull School Trail, you'll be following the eastern part of this old market route. Hull School was near where this trail intersects the North Fork Thornton River Trail, but you won't find any signs of the schoolhouse today.

"It was a small building, but it was right lively," remembered Bessie Compton Woodward. "We had all grades, from the ABCs to American history, and anywhere from 12 to 20 students. We each had a speller, a dictionary, a reader, and geography and arithmetic books. There was no fussin' or fightin' or carryin' on at school in those days. If you didn't behave, the teacher would punish you by making you stand on one foot on a stick of wood, or you'd have to stand in the corner. Then the kids would tease you about that at recess. And your parents' motto was, 'If you're not going to learn, you might as well stay home and work.' "

The Hull School in the 1930s.

Bessie lived a quarter mile east of the school. Her family had a large barn, a hen house, and a spring house in addition to their six-room home. Pastureland, orchards, and fields enclosed by stone fences surrounded the house. The Compton family raised almost everything they needed, and they sold apples, cattle, grain, and twists of tobacco.

Bessie and her mother made the twists and sold them at ten for a dollar. "On a damp day you'd pile the tobacco leaves and cover them with a cloth. Then you'd stem the leaf and fold it over to make it narrow, wrap a nice leaf on the outside of it, and twist it." These twists were bought as chewing tobacco.

The farm work and housework were demanding, but there was still time for fun. As Bessie grew up she enjoyed picnics, Sunday afternoon horseback rides up the mountain, and evening walks with other young people. And there were dances, too.

Sometimes a dance would be held in the school building, sometimes in a home. Once they danced in the Compton's kitchen. Another time their dance floor was a platform built in the yard. People came from miles around and danced all night.

Looking back on her girlhood, Bessie said, "Those really were the good ol' days!"

If you you leave the Hull School Trail and walk along the Thornton Hollow Trail, you'll be near Bessie's girlhood home. You'll see traces of the old roads where Bessie walked, stone fences like the ones her father built, and remnants of the once-flourishing orchards where her brothers worked. But you'll be hard-pressed to conjure up the sounds of banjo tunes and dancing feet.

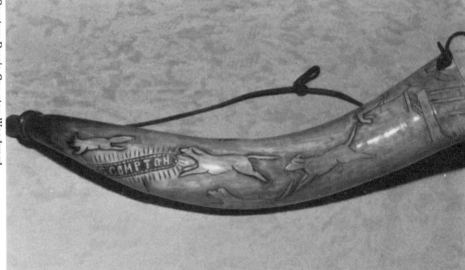

Hand-carved hunting horn that belonged to Bessie's brother.

Road to Pass Mountain Shelter

When Skyline Drive is closed because of snow and ice, Park visitors turned away at the Thornton Gap entrance have an option. They can salvage the day by walking—or cross-country skiing—along the administrative road that leads to the Pass Mountain Hut. The hut is one of the three-sided shelters PATC maintains for Appalachian Trail hikers.

If you follow this road, you'll cross the area where the Panorama Hotel stood between Lee Highway and the mountain's peak. The hotel was on the hill with a view to the west. Below it was the Panorama subdivision, with vacation cottages on separate lots.

Further up the road, you'll pass through land that Barbara Cliser owned in the mid-nineteenth century. She had what was reputed to be the largest and best spring in the area. As a child, Fran Eldred often heard the story of how Union soldiers used the spring at "Aunt Barbara's place" when they camped in the Panorama area. This was probably in 1863. Historian John W. Wayland wrote that "soldiers buzzed like angry hornets in the area of Hawsburg" that summer.

When the Union soldiers left, a local boy went with them, but there is disagreement about the circumstances. One story is that he created a family scandal by running off to be a Yankee drummer boy; another is that he was conscripted and forced to accompany the Union army.

Near Panorama, looking toward Hogback and Mt. Marshall, 1929.

In due time, the boy returned safely from his adventure. He grew up, married a local girl, and became a respected citizen of Rappahannock County. The details of his "joining" the Union army, never widely known, are another of Shenandoah's secrets.

Some Hazel Country Trails

"Hazel Country" was notorious as a stronghold of the mountain moonshiners—people whose self-preservation required them to be suspicious of strangers. "Even the tax collector didn't go in there!" declared a woman from a hollow a dozen miles miles away. And the 1932 edition of *Guide to Paths in the Blue Ridge* warned hikers to avoid the Hazel region until the local people had been moved out of the Park area. Two years earlier, a Potomac Appalachian Trail Club excursion had ended with hikers hurrying down Hazel Mountain after brush alongside the trail was set afire to "encourage" them to leave.

"If somebody from Nicholson Hollow came into Hazel, they'd better know somebody there or have somebody with them that was known in Hazel. And vice versa."
— a former Hazel Hollow resident

Today's hikers, though, can enjoy Hazel Country's well-developed trail system without such added excitement. If you walk down the Hazel Mountain Trail, you'll see remnants of apple orchards planted by families that once lived along its length. And halfway down the mountain, you'll come to a trail that follows one of the area's earliest transportation routes. Built as a "rolling road," it led from Pine Hill Gap to the road through Thornton Gap. Known for many years as the Old Hazel Road, it's now called the Hazel Trail.

People began settling along the Old Hazel Road soon after it was built. By the time the land was condemned for the Park, farms lined both sides. They belonged to the Clark, Atkins, Jenkins, Dodson, and Berry families, among others.

Gilbert Berry spent his boyhood on a farm not far south of today's Hazel Mountain Trail. His family's log home was about a mile below Skyline Drive. He often followed the Old Hazel Road north to Lee Highway, riding horseback with a sack of corn for a saddle. After his corn was ground at the mill near Sperryville, he returned home, riding atop his bag of meal.

Gilbert also traveled that old route with his father, James Adrian Berry. They hauled loads of bark they had peeled from hemlock and chestnut oak to the highway and then across the mountain to the tannery in Luray. To slow the wagon on the steeper descents, Gilbert's father would cut down a tree and tie it behind the wagon to act as an extra brake.

In the 1980s, Gilbert Berry loved to take friends and relatives to the site of the farm his family sold before the Park was established. He'd point out the level area where the family flailed their wheat to separate the grain from the chaff. And he'd find a pile of blackened rocks and explain how they had been heated in a fire and then dropped into half a barrel filled with water to bring it to a boil for scalding hogs at butchering time.

"You'd stack up a layer of logs and cover it with rocks, then lay on another layer of logs going the other way. You'd put more rocks on top of that and keep on layering it up real high. Then you'd set it on fire. By the time the wood had all burned down into coals those rocks would be hot enough to make the water boil. You'd shovel them into the barrel and they'd hiss and steam," he explained.

As a young boy, Gilbert attended the Hazel School. It stood at the western side of the intersection of the Hazel Mountain Trail and Sam's Ridge Trail. You can still see pieces of tin roofing and part of its stone foundation there. The Hazel Church was diagonally opposite the school, but hardly a trace of it can be found today.

That the people of this area were both churchgoers and moonshiners is not a contradiction. Most mountain men made brandy or corn liquor for sale and for family use—some of it for medicinal purposes. (One cold remedy was made by boiling ginger with whiskey and sugar.)

During prohibition, some moonshiners in areas accessible by automobile—as Hazel Hollow was—did sell their product to

Jack Dodson and his family. Jack's whiskey had a distinctive flavor that was recognized for miles around.

bootleggers. But the hollow's legendary moonshiner, Jack Dodson, had only one customer from outside the area: a hiker who bought the two-quart fruit jars of colorless liquid for his own use.

One of the most pleasant trails in Hazel Country is the Catlett Mountain Trail. It branches off the Hazel Mountain Trail in a fertile area once known locally as Sandy Flat. It leads west, passing through overgrown orchards and farmland, and eventually intersects the Hannah Run Trail.

Generations of hikers on the Catlett Mountain Trail have wondered about the enormous hole near this intersection. Gilbert Berry remembered when it was even larger and deeper and had a wooden frame to reinforce its sides. He knew its story, too.

In the late nineteenth and early twentieth century, Nathan Jenkins spent all his spare time excavating there, looking for gold. Whenever he could afford to, he paid his neighbors to help him dig. Even now the ground nearby sparkles with the bits of mica that spurred him on.

We smile at this today, thinking how gullible Jenkins was. But Virginia was once the third leading gold-producing state in the nation. Gold valued at more than $1,500,000 was sent to the U.S. mint between 1829 and 1860—some of it from the very county where the mountain man was digging. But it was the moonshiners' "liquid gold," not ore from Nathan Jenkins' mine, that made Hazel Country famous.

Ned Johnson, of Rappahannock County, used to tell the story of twin brothers who cut tanbark in Hazel Country. On a summer day, they were carrying armfuls of bark they had stacked earlier and were loading it onto their wagon. One of the twins was horrified to see a rattlesnake on the load his brother had just picked up. Because he stammered, the man couldn't shout a warning, so he grabbed the snake and killed it with his bare hands!

Hannah Run Trail

The steep, rugged Hannah Run Trail takes you past several old mountain homesites. For the first mile below Skyline Drive, the trail is one built by the Park Service. But beyond the signpost, where it turns sharply right, the route is one the mountain people used long before there was a park.

You'll find the first homesite soon after you cross Hannah Run, still a small stream at this elevation. Look for fences, collapsed outbuildings, and the ruins of a large cabin with a lean-to kitchen across the back. Look for two more homesites on your left within the next quarter mile.

As you continue, watch for apple trees, chestnut stumps, gateposts, and fragments of old fences. If you look carefully as the trail parallels the main branch of Hannah Run on gently descending ground, you might see faint, abandoned side roads. Once, they led to other farms, but few signs of them can be found today.

The abandoned homesites you see along the trail today are only part of a much larger community—a "suburb" of Nicholson Hollow, which lay along the Hughes River at the foot of the Hannah Run Trail.

Looking up Hannah Run Trail toward Albert Nicholson's house.

Mountain men beside a springhouse in the Hannah Run area.

Albert Nicholson and his son, in the mid-1930s.

Corbin Cabin Cutoff Trail

Today's Corbin Cabin Cutoff Trail was the route Virgil Corbin took when he was water boy for the construction crew on Skyline Drive. Every morning, 15-year-old Virgil walked from his family's cabin in Nicholson Hollow to the mountain crest. There, for 20 cents an hour, he carried spring water to the road workers. In the evening he walked the two miles back down the trail, passing the farmsites of two of his Nicholson relatives as he neared his home in the Hollow. (If you make this hike in the winter, you may want to explore the old sites as you pass them.)

Virgil's father, George Corbin, built the family's cabin when he was a young man, locating it a stone's throw from the cabin where he grew up. He hewed the logs and joists from chestnut, rived out and dressed the floor lumber with a drawknife, and hand rived the chestnut shakes with a froe. The finished cabin had a main room and a loft.

Shenandoah National Park Archives

The George Corbin family.

111

Later, George Corbin added a lean-to kitchen across the back. He had recently put a metal roof on the cabin and was building a lean-to bedroom on one end when he had to vacate because of the Park. He'd made these improvements believing that the government would allow the people to remain in their homes. Ironically, the price he received for his land was almost the same as the cost of the materials used in remodeling the cabin.

During the next two decades the cabin slowly deteriorated. Then, in the early 1950s, the Potomac Appalachian Trail Club received Park permission to restore it for use by hikers.

A winter visit to this cabin can give you an idea of the discomfort some mountain families faced. It's heated only by a fireplace, but PATC's volunteers made Corbin Cabin more weather-tight, so you'll be warmer than young Virgil was. Years after he left Nicholson Hollow, he still remembered how snow blew through the cracks between the logs.

As you carry wood for the fireplace and kitchen stove and lug buckets of water from the nearby Hughes River, you'll be literally following in the footsteps of the Corbin family. But they did it year after year instead of for a weekend, and they had livestock to look after and the fields and garden to plant and cultivate, too. For us, a week or a weekend at Corbin Cabin is recreation. But for Virgil and his family, living here year in and year out was just plain hard work.

The restored Corbin Cabin in 1971.

Corbin Hollow Trail

The Corbin Hollow Trail runs along Broken Back Run between Old Rag Road and Weakley Hollow Road. Both of these roads were important to the people who lived in this area. The Weakley Hollow Road led to the store at Nethers where they traded their homemade baskets for salt pork, and the Old Rag Road to led to Skyland. The people of Corbin Hollow depended on Skyland for their livelihood. Some cut firewood for the resort or worked in its gardens. Others sold the baskets they made or fruit they grew and wild berries they picked. And, a few went there to beg.

Unlike the mountain people in other areas, most of the Corbin Hollow people were unable to support themselves on their land, and some lived in poverty. A 1930 letter from L. Ferdinand Zerkel describes the worst cabin in the hollow:

> I recall it contained a single room of about 10' by 12' on the entrance floor from a very rude porch and a half-story room above entered through a square opening by means of a ladder from the outside. The place is built of logs with clay chinking and no exterior weatherboarding or stripping and no interior ceiling, strips, or plaster. The lower room contained a large wood bed or bunk and a small iron cook stove and two rude chairs and a small nailed-up table. . . .
>
> The bed was in use as a work-bench for the making of baskets—these all of the same near-round half-bushel style. . . . the half-story attic room was sleeping quarters for three partly-grown children and provided a place for storing onions and herbs and likely some home-grown tobacco. . . .
>
> The cabin . . . is devoid of glass. For windows, a form of porthole in the logs (its outside size about four times its inside size) admits light and air and is or was the lookout and place through which to shoot an approaching enemy—one such, at least, having been killed not many yards from this cabin. . . .

The writer went on to emphasize that this was an extreme case. The press, though, focused attention on the destitution of a few homes in Corbin Hollow. Some people whose families lost their property to the Park believe its boosters deliberately portrayed the mountain people in this light. The reason? So popular opinion would favor removing them "for their own good" and allay criticisms of the condemnation of their land.

As you walk along the trail, observe how much narrower this hollow is than others you have walked through. Notice how steep and rocky it is. Even today, Corbin Hollow seems less hospitable than the other hollows in the Park.

Esther and Jordan Nicholson, Corbin Hollow youngsters.

Corbin Hollow cabin interiors.

115

Mrs. Bailey Nicholson.

Above: The Eddie Nicholson family made baskets to sell at Skyland. An ax to cut down a white oak tree, a maul and wooden wedges to split the log into eights, and a "whittlin' knife" to cut the wood into fine strips were all that was needed to make these baskets. Below: Fennel Corbin.

Two Corbin Hollow mothers. Above: Dicey Corbin and her daughter, Betty. Below: Blanch Nicholson and her son, LeRoy.

Corbin Hollow children. Above: Boy in a straw hat. Below: Estelle and Florine Nicholson.

Virgie Corbin, about 16 years old.

Corbin Hollow kitchen scenes.

121

The Nicholson Hollow Trail

The Nicholson Hollow Trail follows old roads from Skyline Drive to the Park boundary, 5.8 miles east. Less than two miles from the Drive you'll reach Corbin Cabin (see p. 112).

Twenty or so families lived along the Hughes River below Corbin Cabin. They had gardens, fields, orchards, and pastures on land they had cleared along both sides of the river. The men farmed, hunted, trapped, and gathered ginseng to sell, and some of them worked at trades. In the early 1930s, four were stonemasons, two were carpenters, and three made baskets. Many others worked in lumbering or as day laborers. And in hidden spots near constant water sources, they ran their stills, sure of a market at Pollock's Skyland resort.

You can see chimneys and other evidence of homesites as you walk along the Nicholson Hollow Trail today, but across the Hughes River the most impressive ruin is just out of sight. It was once the home of Aaron Nicholson, a farmer who owned about 75 acres but who claimed to own all the land he could see "from

The Aaron Nicholson house in Nicholson Hollow.

Shenandoah National Park Archives

peak to peak." He was born in 1830, one of the fourth generation of Nicholsons to live in the hollow. When he "retired" from farming, he deeded most of his land to his children and spent the rest of his life gardening and making split-oak baskets. If you find the Aaron Nicholson site, look for remnants of his large, two-story house with chimneys at either end, a vegetable pit, and the stone fence that surrounded his garden.

As you continue along the Nicholson Hollow Trail you'll be following the route to the store and gristmill at Nethers. Before Prohibition, the Nicholson men used this route to transport hundreds of gallons of apple brandy out of the hollow each year, as well.

The brandy they distilled from Milam apples was said to be the finest in the country. Nicholson Hollow men took it to settlements as far as twenty-five miles away. Try to imagine the "processions consisting of several keg-laden mules led by two giant mountaineers, cradling their long rifles in their arms and brought up at the rear by two more." Those must have been prosperous years in the hollow—brandy sold for two dollars a gallon then.

Adam Nicholson.

Two Nicholson Hollow homes.

Nicholson Hollow farmer with a "slide" full of cornstalks.

The Nicholson Hollow School and the Hughes River Church stood near the Hannah Run Trail intersection. The school, a typical log cabin, was also used for religious services until the church was built. Before Skyland guests hired a teacher in the late 1920s, education often had been unavailable. School was in session only four months during the fifteen years ending in 1918. As was true throughout Virginia, the literacy rate in the hollow had decreased significantly in the decades following the Civil War.

Nicholson Hollow is now one of the most publicized areas of the Park. George Pollock wrote about the hollow and its people in *Skyland*, and it was the "Needles" community in Mandel and Sherman's *Hollow Folk* (1933). Pollock's treatment of the mountain people was patronizing. And according to researchers Charles and Nancy Perdue, the authors of *Hollow Folk* "were unable to view the mountain people in anything resembling an objective manner and the result is at best insensitive reporting and at worst falsified data."

The Perdues' well-documented research shows the people of Nicholson Hollow as part of the mainstream of rural America. They bought and sold land, fought in both the Civil War and World War I, voted, visited nearby towns (and sometimes cities), and had conventional moral standards. But by the time social scientists and reporters came into the hollow, the people were suffering from the effects of the chestnut blight, a severe drought, and government restrictions on their traditional ways of making a living. Also, as the Perdues point out, Prohibition had recently "turned an honest occupation into a criminal act and honest men into outlaws."

Because a stranger in the hollow might be a revenue agent, suspicion of "foreigners" grew. Some of those foreigners did come into the hollow to look for moonshine stills. But others came to look for something to write about—something that would capture the public interest in the new Shenandoah National Park. A few of these writers portrayed the people accurately, but most were looking for a colorful story.

Dr. Roy L. Sexton collection, PATC Archives

Three generations: the Newt and Albert Nicholsons.

White Oak Canyon

White Oak Canyon's falls—six of them—have been a hikers' destination for generations. Today's well-maintained trail, which passes all of White Oak Run's cascades and waterfalls, was built by the Park Service. But in Skyland's early days, the guests followed ax-blazed paths through heavy forest to camp deep in the canyon and swim in pools below the falls. Later, they approached the falls by way of the Old Rag Road to what was known as "middle bridge." There, proprietor George Pollock had dammed White Oak Run to form a swimming pool and had built a changing shelter.

The area where the White Oak Canyon Trail intersects the Limberlost Trail and the White Oak Road was once known as Comer's Deadening. Here the settler "deadened" the trees, killing them by girdling their trunks with his ax. The next spring, the sun could reach the ground through the bare branches, and he was able to plant his "new ground" without the effort of clearing it.

Swimming pool in White Oak Canyon, about 1928.

Dr. Roy L. Sexton, PATC Archives

Changing house at the White Oak Canyon swimming pool.

If you hike the full length of the trail to the canyon's mouth, you will be in an area settled long before crops were planted in Comer's deadening. Germans came here as early as the mid-1720s. They came from Germanna, the "company town" of German iron workers Governor Spotswood founded in an effort to establish an iron industry in Virginia. When their indentures ran out, the workers left Germanna. Most of them settled near today's town of Madison, but according to historian Jean Stephenson, some made their way as far north as the mouth of White Oak Canyon.

128

Old Rag Circuit

Climbing Old Rag is such a popular weekend activity that late-comers often have to park nearly a mile from the trailhead. Youth groups and hiking clubs, families and couples are drawn to the challenges of the rocky summit with its panoramic views. It has been that way for years.

In the early days, groups of Skyland visitors followed blazed paths to Old Rag's summit and camped out. Their experience, however, was different from that of today's overnighters. First of all, they were unencumbered by packs—their food, water, bedding, and personal gear were carried by mountain men hired by the resort's proprietor. After dinner (no dehydrated foods for them!) they washed the dishes in water that had collected in potholes in the rock. Then, unhampered by the rules today's heavy use of the Park has made necessary, they sat around the campfire. Finally, they bedded down in what George Pollock described as "cozy nooks enclosed by towering rock formations, and heavily carpeted with soft moss six to eight inches deep."

In the morning they woke to the smell of freshly brewed coffee and watched the sun rise over the Piedmont before they hiked down from the summit. Then they had breakfast at one of the mountain cabins before hiking back to Skyland. It wasn't backpacking, and it certainly wasn't roughing it. But what an adventure it must have been!

Virginia's Senator Harry F. Byrd, Sr., was introduced to Old Rag on one of these overnight hikes when he was quite young. So impressed was he that he later made annual pilgrimages to the mountain. Byrd climbed Old Rag on his birthday for over half a century. In his later years, he was driven to the Old Rag Shelter and walked the last mile to the summit from there, accompanied by his black cocker spaniel.

Shenandoah National Park was important to Byrd. As Governor during the early years of the Park movement and later as Senator, he was involved in its formation. The Visitor Center at Big Meadows is named for him, as are hiker huts throughout the Park. The large stone shelter half a mile southwest of Old Rag's summit was the first of four stone shelters that he gave to the Park.

It was dedicated in 1961, on the Senator's 74th birthday. Since then, many a hiker has taken refuge from stormy weather in "Byrd's Nest Shelter #1."

Hikers' equipment has changed since the early days, but the problem is still the same. (The sign is the same, too.)

Though hikers are sometimes caught unprepared by bad weather on Old Rag, the local people kept a close eye on the mountain and knew its moods. A woman who worked among the people told how a man would say, "Th' fog's ah-liftin' on the Rag. It's ah-goin' ter clear." And it would. Or a child would say, "See th' fog a-rollin' down the Rag. Hit's ah-goin' ter rain." And it would. (When the mountain was covered with fog, school would be dismissed so the pupils could reach home safely before the streams rose from storm run-off.)

As you hike the Old Rag Circuit, pause to read the concrete signpost near where the Weakley Hollow Road and the Old Rag Road intersect. You'll be standing on the site of the former mountain community known as Old Rag Post Office. The center of Old Rag P.O., as it was sometimes called, was the flat area close to the signpost. It was near here that the area's first house was built in 1750. By the 1930s, homes were scattered in a half-mile-wide belt that stretched for a mile or so along the Weakley Hollow and Old Rag roads. The community had a one-room school and a one-room meeting house, but its focal point was the small log building that served as both store and post office.

Old Rag Store and Post Office.

131

William A. Brown was the storekeeper and postmaster. The mail was brought on horseback from the town of Syria three times a week. But Brown drove seven miles to the store in Nethers to exchange eggs, rabbits, and produce the local people traded at his store for coffee, sugar, and other staple products that stocked his shelves.

Education was important to the people of Old Rag. The community had a school by 1871, and the term was nine months in the 1920s.

In the early 1930s, the teacher at the Old Rag School sponsored a "pie social" to raise money to pay the man who'd taken the pupils to the county fair in his truck. Nine young girls brought pies they had baked, and the young men came to buy them as they were auctioned off. Although who had baked each pie was supposed to be a secret, it wasn't. Each fellow bought the pie baked by the girl he was "talking to," and the couples sat down at classroom desks to eat them. (The auction raised $3.75.)

Today, there's little left to hint of the settlement that started in "the flat." And when we see the lush greenery of Old Rag today, it's hard to imagine that in the drought-ravaged summer of

Postmaster William A. Brown.

Two of Postmaster Brown's granddaughters.

133

A home near Old Rag.

1930 the mountain burned for weeks. Raging turf fires burned fences throughout the area and consumed 30 or 40 cords of tanbark Will Woodward and Ashby Jenkins had cut and stacked.

The cornfields planted on the steep mountain slopes west of the hollow returned to forest long ago, but you can see apple trees and stone fences along the Weakley Hollow Fire Road. And at a wide turn in the Saddle Trail below the wooden shelter, you might glimpse oval leaves of periwinkle growing among field stones that mark the graves in the Old Rag Cemetery.

Rose River Loop

As you walk down the Rose River Road through Dark Hollow, you'll be following the route of a mid-nineteenth century turnpike. Because it led to the railroad terminal in the Piedmont town of Gordonsville, it was called the Gordonsville Pike. But its official name was the Blue Ridge Turnpike.

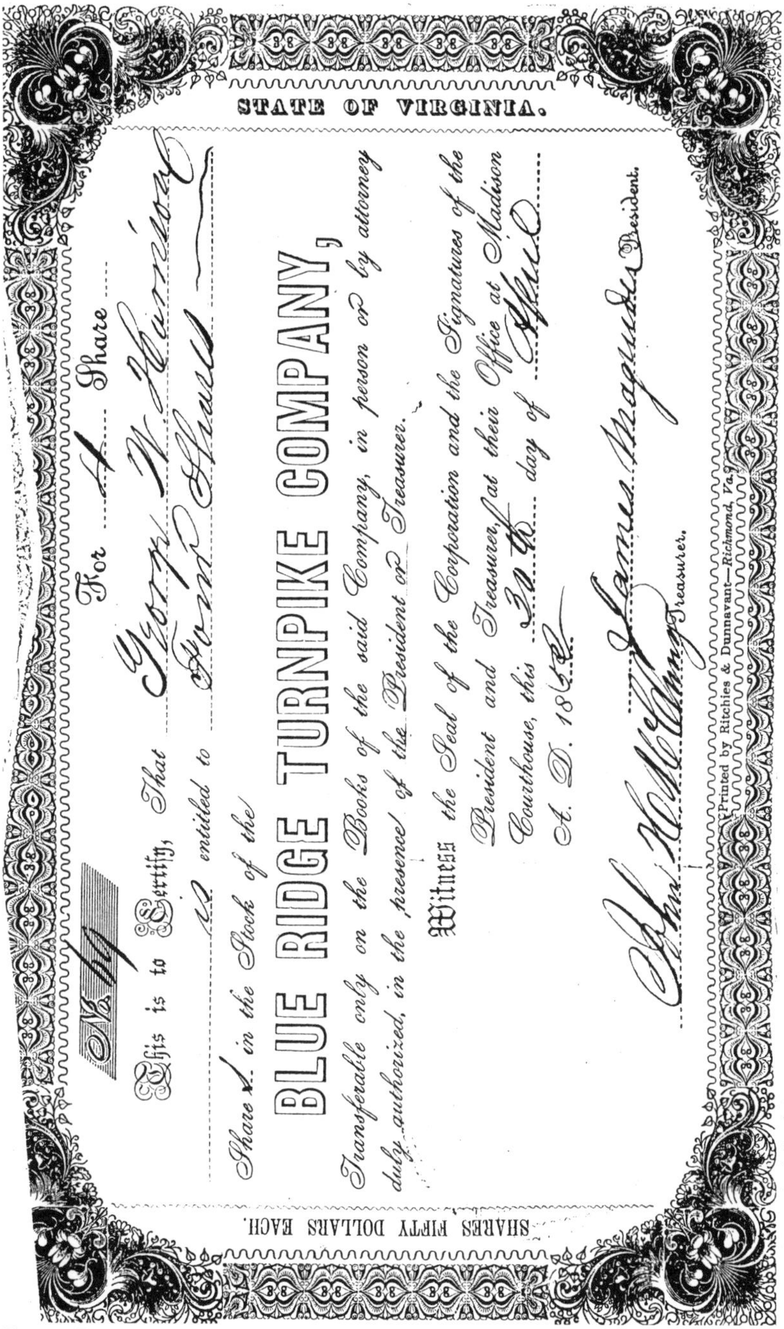

Turnpike company stock certificate.

STATE OF VIRGINIA.

For ___ 1 ___ Share

This is to Certify, That ___ George W. Harrison ___ is entitled to ___ one ___ Share ___ in the Stock of the

BLUE RIDGE TURNPIKE COMPANY,

Transferable only on the Books of the said Company, in person or by attorney duly authorized, in the presence of the President or Treasurer.

Witness the Seal of the Corporation and the Signatures of the President and Treasurer, at their Office at Madison Courthouse, this ___ 20th ___ day of ___ April ___ A. D. 184__

James Maqui__ President.

W. M. M____ Treasurer.

SHARES FIFTY DOLLARS EACH.

Virginia Historical Society

135

Paschal Graves and his son James Madison Graves, of nearby Syria, were in charge of constructing the section of the road that included the east slope of the Blue Ridge. After the rocks were blasted out and piled along the roadway, laborers broke them up with sledge hammers. Then, horse- or mule-driven scrapers graded the road's surface. When it was finished, the elder Graves opened an ordinary to serve travelers, beginning a family tradition of innkeeping. (His descendants operate the well-known Graves Mountain Lodge in Syria, not far outside the Park's eastern boundary.)

For decades, this turnpike road was an important transmountain route. Shenandoah Valley farmers drove herds of livestock and flocks of turkeys along its length. Mountain men used it to haul their wagonloads of tanbark or chestnuts and apples to market, too.

During the Civil War, Stonewall Jackson's army crossed the Blue Ridge on the Gordonsville Pike through Fishers Gap—an army so large that it is said to have stretched all the way from the Shenandoah River across the Blue Ridge and down what we now call the Rose River Road.

Although it did not operate as a turnpike after the Civil War, when Jackson's soldiers removed the toll gates, the road continued to be known as the Gordonsville Pike. It was used until the Park closed it to transmountain traffic.

A young man wrote about the devastation of the chestnut blight he witnessed when he hiked through Fishers Gap in 1926: ". . . I passed through a scene impressive in its aspect of desolation, and also a tribute to the destructive powers of the chestnut blight. This section must at one time have been entirely a pure chestnut grove. Now every tree was dead. All the trees had been uprooted and lay flat on the ground. The rains and the snow had washed away the dead bark and bleached the trunks a grayish white. No underbrush of any sort grew there. The area was as free from tree growth as are some of the western plains. These chestnuts were of tremendous size — a foot or two or three feet in diameter. Now it is a graveyard of giant trees. . . . The area was easily two square miles."

Above: **Tom Breeden's family lived at the head of Dark Hollow.**
Below: **Charley Smith's house in Dark Hollow.**

Elsie Cave with her children, Gladys, Johnny, and Dennis.

The Dark Hollow Church, built around 1920 by G.A. Cave and his sons, across the Gordonsville Pike from their home. The ship's bell in the belfry was said to have been donated by President Hoover, whose fishing camp was only a few miles away.

138

A Dark Hollow family.

In the 1930s, the Lariloba Mining Company, which mined copper "on and off but never very successfully," owned the land on the north side of the Rose River Road. A mine employee later claimed that this company was involved in a stock market fraud. He said shareholders were told the copper had been exhausted when actually the shaft to a productive vein had been blocked up.

A few of the mine owners planned to buy back the stock after the price had fallen substantially and then reopen the shaft, pretending to have found a new vein of copper. But the plan backfired when the mining company's land was condemned for the Park. This story has become part of the area's folklore, and like so much of the oral tradition, it can be neither proved nor disproved.

A Shenandoah Valley cattleman owned the land on the south side of the Rose River Road. Mountain families lived on his land and also on the Lariloba tract. There were Breedens, Woodwards, and Burackers, but the most common surname in the area was Cave. The first of the Caves to live here came to work as a tollgate keeper on the turnpike. His descendants stayed to farm the land and haul out wood and tanbark.

You can find remnants of homesites along the road and a well-kept cemetery on the right side about half a mile from Skyline Drive. A half mile beyond it is the site of the Dark Hollow Church, sometimes used as a school as well as for religious services.

Just before a steel bridge, detour up the Dark Hollow Trail to see the cascading Dark Hollow Falls. Then return and take the blue-blazed Rose River Loop Trail. It leaves the road on the downhill side of the bridge and goes left.

After about a mile, you'll cross Hogcamp Branch, the stream you've been following, and shortly reach the site of an old copper mine. It was worked by different companies at various times beginning in the mid-nineteenth century. Its three shafts have been filled, but you can see the pile of mine tailings and the concrete base where the air compressor for the miners' pneumatic drills was anchored.

The Blue Ridge Copper Company, which began operations here in 1902, also built a two-story log house, a powder house, a blacksmith shop, and other small buildings nearby. Although the mine yielded rich ore, extracting it from the narrow veins proved too expensive, and the company closed down.

After you explore the copper mine area, continue along the Rose River Loop Trail to return to Skyline Drive.

Big Meadows Ramble

The openness of Big Meadows invites exploration. As you ramble there, allow your eyes to "ramble," too, looking for signs of the people who once lived on the meadow. Start by following the clear but unmarked trails leading east to find the most evidence of old homesites and CCC activity.*

During the years since the Park was established, the meadow has grown smaller and smaller. Without cattle grazing and people cutting firewood, the forest has slowly but steadily reclaimed the open land. If it weren't for annual mowings by the Park Service, the meadow would have disappeared long ago.

Beyond the clearing, where the forest is reclaiming the meadow, you can find foundations and cellars of several mountain cabins that once stood beneath the open sky. Another homesite, this one closer to the Visitor Center and to the northern edge of the open meadow, can be spotted only by its non-native vegetation. In mid-April, daffodils planted by a mountain woman decades ago still bloom in flowerbeds there.

On the northeastern border of today's meadow you can find vestiges of a landscape nursery. Here, CCC recruits at Camp Fechner grew trees and shrubs to use for landscaping Skyline Drive. Other evidence of the CCC is meager, but as you ramble, you may find the foundation outlines of some of the camp's buildings.

Well into the woods, northeast of today's meadow, are some low cliffs. Initials and dates carved in the rock of the cliffs and now nearly hidden by lichens probably were made by Skyland visitors long before the Shenandoah National Park was contemplated.

Below the cliffs are trash piles, no doubt of CCC origin. You'll find broken china and canning jars, tools, and parts of vehicles at the old homesites. But at the trash piles below the cliffs you'll find truck tires, metal roofing, barrels, and similar items. You may find it interesting to look through the discards of an earlier time, but remember that it's against the law to remove any of these artifacts. They are preserved by the Park as "historic trash."

---

*Walking in the meadow is a pleasure in every season, but late fall through early spring is the best time to look for the things we mention here. If you are not experienced in walking "off-trail," however, you would be advised not to try looking without a guide, since the things we describe are not readily seen. In warm weather, the Park often schedules naturalist-led hikes.

Shenandoah National Park Archives

At various times during World War II, "considerable numbers" of military forces were in the Park. The base camp of the Engineer Replacement Training Center was at Big Meadows.

Elsewhere in the overgrown area, you may find evidence of modern uses of the former grazing land—a weather station and a physical fitness training course for Park Rangers. But it's the open land that attracts us. And it's the traces of old roads and other hints of the past that add to the pleasure of walking across this grassy, wind-swept mountain meadow.

Trails to Hoover's Camp Rapidan

In today's fast-paced and sophisticated world, it's hard to imagine a President of the United States whose favorite recreation was trout fishing—a president who took state visitors to rough it in a remote setting in Virginia's Blue Ridge Mountains before there was a Park or Skyline Drive. But that's what Herbert Hoover did.

Hoover called his retreat Camp Rapidan. He described it as "a place for weekend rest," but his guests often included legislators and government officials, and he tended to combine work with recreation. More recently known as Camp Hoover, in its day it was also known as "the President's Camp," and local papers referred to it as the "Summer White House" or as a "fishing lodge."

For the most direct route to the site of Camp Rapidan, simply follow Mill Prong Trail the entire way. (It branches off the *AT* a few yards from Skyline Drive at Milam Gap.) The longer route follows the Rapidan Road for 1.5 miles to the horse trail leading to Mill Prong Trail, which will take you to the historic area. If you choose this option, you'll be walking on part of the original "Hoover Highway" from the President's Camp to Thornton Gap. (This road was the drought-relief project that grew into Skyline Drive. See page 29.)

At the camp, you'll find that three rustic buildings have been preserved. (Work began in 1997 to remove interior changes made since the Hoovers' day and to restore the structures' historical authenticity.) One of the buildings is "The President," the cabin where the Hoovers stayed. Just outside it, Mill Prong froths and tumbles over boulders as it rushes to join the Laurel Prong and

Libary of Congress

President Herbert Hoover, near his camp.

143

Lloyd Woodward's farm on the "Hoover Road" near the President's Camp.

form the Rapidan River. Perhaps it was here that Herbert Hoover first mused that trout fishing was a "reminder of human frailty—for all men are equal before fishes."

To the right of "The President," you'll see "The Prime Minister," the cabin where British Prime Minister Ramsey Mac-Donald stayed on an official visit to the U.S. Here at Hoover Camp the two leaders discussed limiting the size of the world's fleets. They hoped to reduce both the drain on national budgets and the threat to world peace they saw in the arms build-up of that earlier day.

The remaining cabin is "The Creel," where two presidential assistants stayed. These three buildings are all that are left of the complex that existed in Hoover's day, when a total of thirteen buildings stood in the area of the President's Camp. A mile to the east was the Marine Camp, where the president's official guard was billeted, and two miles downstream was the Cabinet Camp, used by cabinet members who came to confer with Hoover.

Hoover School.

Today's Hoover Camp, a National Historic Landmark, covers only few acres. But the Hoovers owned a 164-acre tract plus another acre and a half where they established a school for the local children.* It took a company of almost 500 marines to improve the road to the camp, to clear the land and construct the buildings, and to help build trails in the surrounding area. They "worked day and night," and Hoover Camp was ready for the president's first visit just five weeks after the project—part of the marines' training—was begun.

But it had been a grueling job. The marine commander wrote, "It would have been easier to have moved an army of 10,000 men across the Blue Ridge than to have built this camp. I have been amazed to find so wild an area existing here so close to the eastern cities."

---

*Herbert Hoover's Hideaway, by Darwin Lambert (Shenandoah Natural History Association, 1971), tells the complete story of Hoover Camp, the nearby Hoover School, and the people and events associated with both.

If you have the time and energy after exploring Hoover Camp, go south on the Laurel Prong Trail to the Fork Mountain Trail. It was part of the 75-mile trail system built for the pleasure of Hoover and his guests. Follow it to the Fork Mountain Road and turn left to reach the mountain's summit in the wilderness area just outside the Park boundary.

In Hoover's day, there was a fire tower on Fork Mountain, and marines manned it whenever fire danger was high. Visitors from the camp climbed the tower to enjoy the view, and some claimed that with binoculars they could see the Washington Monument.

Today a Federal Aviation Administration relay tower stands on Fork Mountain. It seems an intrusion in a wild, natural area, but, ironically, there is a precedent for this use of the mountain's peak. According to an elderly woman who once lived in the area, heliograph signals—beams of sunlight flashed by a mirror—were sent from this same mountain top during the Civil War.

Although many people fought to keep their mountain property (or to get a better price for it), the Hoovers donated their land to Shenandoah National Park for the future enjoyment of their fellow citizens.

The Graves' Honeymoon Cottage was about a mile from Hoover Camp. Pollock often brought Skyland guests here for a noon meal, and parties of local people rented the cottage as a base camp for horseback trips. (Note telephone line at left. Some of its chestnut poles still stand today.)

Shenandoah National Park Archives

The Trails on Tanners Ridge

You can walk through the Tanners Ridge area on either the Tanners Ridge Road or the Appalachian Trail between Big Meadows and Milam Gap. At the intersection of these routes you'll see a well-tended cemetery, the most easily observable evidence that this was once a settlement. A short distance south on the *AT* is a homesite with a large spring. Notice the fruit trees, fence remnants, and other signs of habitation along the way.

Tanners Ridge was once cleared, part of Big Meadows. Many of the people living there in the first third of the twentieth century were year-long tenants for Shenandoah Valley farmers who grazed cattle on the ridge. The Tanners Ridge Road linked the community to the town of Stanley, a few miles to the west. Beside the road, just past today's Park boundary, was an Episcopal mission with a church and school.

The families who lived on this ridge had an easier life than those who lived in narrow, isolated hollows or on remote mountain slopes. When these families had to leave after the Park's formation, they didn't want to go. People still tell of the man who hanged himself in his barn rather than leave. Although this is a word-of-mouth story, another instance of reluctance to leave Tanners Ridge has been officially documented.

One night in March 1937, the sheriff and his deputies, assisted by Park personnel, evicted a family that refused to leave the land where they had been tenants. Over a period of many years, this family had improved the property with buildings, fences,

147

The forcible eviction on Tanners Ridge.

This wooden marker was erected at the site of a murder on the Tanners Ridge Road. Speaking of the crime, a local man later declared, "I think they kindly had a grudge against one another some way or other over some girls."

and orchards they believed were worth about $1,500 and they claimed equity in the property. Unfortunately, however, the tenant didn't make a claim to the Clerk of the County Court for a share of the landowners' payment. And, in spite of urging by both mission workers and a state official, he refused to sign the occupancy permit that would have allowed his family to stay on the land temporarily. His fear of "signing away his rights" set the stage for the eviction.

For two years, this family lived on borrowed time. Park officials were reluctant to put them out of their home, and whenever an eviction was planned, the family pleaded illness. On one occasion, a CCC doctor brought along to prevent malingering said the father was indeed suffering from influenza and shouldn't be moved.

A former Park Superintendant who was a ranger at the time remembered one of the attempts and the actual eviction:

> Officers go in at night, you know, so as to find everyone home. It was 4 a.m. when we got there, but the lamp in that cabin was lit. We didn't know whether they'd been warned, but everybody was in bed claiming they were sick. Next time we brought a CCC doctor. He examined [the wife] first and pronounced her well, through pregnant. She wouldn't walk, so we picked her up bodily. She started praying, but before we got her out of the house and into the car she'd called us all kinds of names. Then we got [the husband] out —which left five or six large girls who fought like cats. But we had plenty of help. We moved the furniture out, and the CCC crew started tearing the house down. A reporter arrived about then, and the story got quite a spread.

Records show that the family was taken to an almshouse near the town of Stanley. For some time, the head of the family wrote letters to both state and federal officials, without results.

But years later, he and his wife returned to Tanners Ridge, for good. They lie undisturbed in the cemetery there, and Appalachian Trail hikers pass their handsome marker unaware that it represents the long-delayed "last word" in a mountain family's conflict with the government, a dramatic struggle they finally won.

149

Long before development of the Park disrupted the mountain people's lives, an old woman on Tanners Ridge saw it happening. Everyone thought she was mad when she looked eastward across the ridge and swore she saw droves of people and a road being built and machines tearing up the sod on Mr. Long's grazing farm. But years later, when Skyline Drive was under construction, her family and neighbors remembered.

The Staunton River Trail

On the east side of Jones Mountain is a cabin that's been painstakingly restored—and improved by the addition of a skylight—by the Potomac Appalachian Trail Club. To reach the cabin, once the home of Harvey Nichols, enter the Park at its eastern boundary. Then walk the three miles along the Staunton River and Jones Mountain Trails to the cabin. On the way, you'll pass through an area once inhabited by Lillards, Shifletts, McDaniels, and other industrious mountain people.*

At times, many of the local residents worked at Brown's Lumbering Camp, near the trailhead parking area. The camp's mess hall stood between the Staunton River Trail—then a road—and a railroad that paralleled it. The railroad carried the finished lumber out of the mountains to Wolftown and Orange. Logging operations ended in 1925, however, and the tracks were removed a few years later. Meanwhile, some of the local people moved into the camp's abandoned buildings and lived there until the Park was established.

The Staunton River Trail began as a pack horse trail in the mid-1700s. Sometime between 1820 and 1840, slaves built a road with a stone retaining wall along this old route. During World War

---

Lost Trails and Forgotten People, by Tom Floyd (PATC), gives the history of this area beginning in prehistoric times.

II, the Corps of Engineers trained in the Park, building roads, bridges, and machine gun nests in preparation for the Italian campaign. They improved the old road here, using rocks from the slave-built retaining wall to provide a firmer foundation for it.

The railroad that carried logs from the forest to the lumber camp near the Park boundary paralleled the old road near its beginning. The rail line continued up the valley, then ascended the mountain on two Y-shaped switchbacks. The steam-powered loader that lifted cut logs onto the flatcars was located about 1,000 feet above Wilson Run.

Further along the trail were two distilleries that dated back to the years between the Civil War and 1917, when Prohibition took effect in Viriginia. Apple brandy from these government-regulated businesses was shipped out along the old wagon road in 50-gallon barrels then.

But Harvey Nichols, who lived in the Jones Mountain cabin for fifty years, was one of many men who ran illegal stills even before Prohibition to avoid paying excise tax. He, and others like him, smuggled out their whiskey and fruit brandy in two-quart mason jars, hoping to avoid "the revenoors."

Observant hikers may notice the dark green oval leaves of periwinkle covering a large area along the trail. Almost concealed by this spreading "graveyard myrtle" are scores of field stones marking the graves of those who once lived nearby.

Beyond the Jones Mountain Trail intersection, where cabin visitors turn uphill, a sawmill operated in the early 1920s. Another sawmill was located further up the Staunton River Trail beyond the junction with the McDaniel Hollow Trail. Here, you can see a huge pile of lumber and slabs of bark that were removed before the logs were cut into boards. A second slab pile marks the site of yet another sawmill still further up the trail.

These piles of waste wood are the only evidence of the industries that once thrived in this now quiet spot. And the restored Harvey Nichols cabin with the apple trees and flowing spring in its yard is the only mountain home that still stands.

Jones Mountain hides its secrets well.

The Pocosin Road

A short distance down the Pocosin Road, you'll come to Pocosin Cabin. The CCC built it in 1937, and the Potomac Appalachian Trail Club maintains it for the use of hikers (on a reservation basis).

A mountain woman lived in a cabin near here long before the Park was envisioned. When two young women hikers stopped to chat with her, she invited them to stay for dinner. She prepared cornbread and apple butter, cooked onions, stewed dried apples, and buttermilk for her visitors. They were impressed by her hospitality—which was typical of the mountain people—as well as by the opportunity to see how the local people lived.

The old woman's possessions included an umbrella, a clock, a rifle, and a banjo—all in easy view. The cabin was clean and tidy. The main room had a bed in one corner and a large stone fireplace with jars of fruit filling the mantel. The table and benches where the visitors ate were in the kitchen.

Further down the Pocosin Road, where it intersects the Pocosin Trail, is the site of "Upper Pocosin," an Episcopal mission.

Shenandoah National Park Archives

The mission worker's cabin after the mission closed.

You can still see the ruin of the mission worker's cabin and what remains of the stone church. Before this church was built, services were held in the frame schoolhouse-chapel. Nothing remains of the barn or the clothing bureau, where donated clothing was sold at low prices.

It was 1904 when a young minister ventured into what was then known as "Dark Pocosan" and built the schoolhouse-chapel. At first, many of the local people were opposed to the mission because they feared it would mean an end to their stillhouses. (Religious organizations were at the forefront of a temperance movement that was sweeping the state.) Threats were made on the young minister's life, and the carpenters he hired to build the schoolhouse-chapel were driven away.

But the minister was a brave man, and he eventually won the people over. He once went up to a mountain man's house and introduced himself, saying, "I hear you want to kill me." The mountain man respected this kind of courage, and the two became good friends.

Before Pocosin Mission was built, men in the area spent their Sundays drinking and hunting. But it was "a rare thing to hear the crack of a rifle in these parts on a Sunday" after the mission's presence began to affect the local people's lives.

A young woman who spent a month at the mission in 1914 wrote of listening to the mountain people's stories of the days before the mission was built: "It is said that in those days there was never a gathering of any kind but what there was apt to be terrible fighting, brought about of course by the fact that on these occasions they indulged in moonshine whiskey." There was still fighting and drinking in spite of the mission's influence, however. The young writer reported that she knew of eight or ten fights resulting from drinking in just a few weeks.

The local people were always welcome at the mission worker's home, and it became a center of community life. Once a week, young people from miles around met there to enjoy an evening of games, and people of all ages came to listen to music on the victrola.

Work at Pocosin Mission continued until the Park became a reality. As the time drew closer for the people to leave the hollow for the "outside world," the workers made an effort to acquaint them with that world. Once, they took the children to Charlottesville, where they were treated to chocolate milk and ice cream and saw a movie as guests of the mayor. Then they had a tour of a C&O Railroad train and a brief ride. Finally, the mission workers gave each child ten cents to spend at the dime store, and the older girls visited a department store and rode on the elevator. What a lot of excitement in one day!

Several months later the mission worker wrote, "It is hard to realize that in a few weeks those rugged mountainsides will be bereft of all their dwellers, that there will be no more the echo of school bells and church bells. . . ."

If you explore the old mission site, look for the small cemetery adjoining the Pocosin Trail. Perhaps some of those who once visited the mission workers and listened to their victrola lie beneath the field stone grave markers almost hidden in the periwinkle here.

Dry Run Road

When you start down today's Dry Run Road, you're in Dean territory. James Dean, patriarch of the Dean clan, bought land here in the mid-1800s, and his family had spread throughout the area by the time the Park was established.* He and many of his descendants are buried in the family cemetery near the Drive.

About a quarter mile below Skyline Drive you will see a large boulder on the north bank of Dry Run Road. It appears to point left, across the road. The Dean Mountain School, which for many years was used for Sunday services as well as classes, stood just south of this landmark.

Other families besides the Deans lived in this area— Meadows, Shiffletts, Lams, Hensleys, and Breedens. Irene Breeden Eppard lived near the foot of the Dry Run Road, where it was known as "Burnt Rock Road." Years earlier, a huge boulder at the edge of the road made it difficult to drive a wagon past, and all

---

*See The Dean Mountain Story, by Gloria Dean (PATC) for an account of the family's life during those eight years.

efforts to dig it out failed. Finally, someone thought of a solution. Wood was gathered and a fire was built on the rock. The neighbors took turns tending the fire, keeping it burning all night. The next day they poured water on the rock, and with a great hissing and popping it cracked into pieces that were easily removed from the roadway. From then on, the Breedens and their neighbors spoke of "Burnt Rock Road."

Of the nine children in the Breeden family, only one was a boy. Irene remembered having to help with the heavy chores. "Many a day I've gone out in the field ahead of the plow to grub out the locusts that had grown up," she said. She also helped care for the horses and cut wood. Sometimes she would "man" the cross-cut saw with her father, Doc Breeden, and together they would fell trees and chop off the branches.

The next step was to harness a horse to a lumbering tool called a "grab"—a chain that ended with a hook and was looped around the log. The horse would then drag the log to the sawmill that had been set up on the Breeden's land. It took a double grab and two horses to manage large logs.

Dean men at sawmill.

A "grab" used in hauling logs to the sawmill.

At the sawmill site, workmen used a "cant hook" to roll the log up the skid and to turn it while the steam-powered rotary blade ripped off the bark. Then they would guide the squared log along the carriage and a board would be sliced off with each pass. Irene's father used whatever boards he needed; the rest were hauled to Elkton in a four-horse wagon and sold. Doc Breeden (named after the doctor who brought him into the world) also sold bark to the tanneries in Elkton.

"We sold milk, eggs, butter, and broiler roosters at the store in Elkton, too," Irene remembered. "We didn't often eat eggs or butter—we saved them back to sell." The family had three cows and a flock of chickens. The children called the Plymouth Rock hens "domino chickens" because of their speckled black and white markings.

The Breeden children went to the Maple Springs School, and the family attended the Hensley Church, both outside the present Park boundary. (Irene met her husband, Roy, at the Hensley Church, and they did most of their courting on the walk between there and her house.) Many people who lived on the mountain attended the the Hensley Church, especially during the revivals. G. A. Cave walked all the way from his home in Dark Hollow each day for three weeks to preach at the revivals.

Thinking about life on the mountain she left in 1936, Irene said, "There was plenty of time to go where you wanted to go and to sit and talk with your neighbors. You could work half a day and visit the other half, then go back in time to milk the cows and have supper. Those were real good old days."

"Better than now," her husband agreed. "Better than now."

The Rocky Mount Trail

The Rocky Mount Trail passes through a steep and rugged area that was the scene of a massive five-day search in 1943. It all began late one Monday afternoon in May when four-year-old Doris Dean wandered into the woods near her home at the foot of the Blue Ridge. Though her slightly older brothers immediately reported her missing, Mrs. Dean wasn't able to find the child. The father combed the mountainside when he returned from work a short time later, and neighbors soon joined the search.

Doris Dean

PATC Archives

Late that night, the family asked for help from the conscientious objectors stationed at a Civilian Public Service (CPS) Camp about ten miles away. With lanterns in hand, eight men from the camp joined Mr. Dean, spacing themselves a dozen or so feet apart to sweep the woods on either side of the cow path where Doris had last been seen. All night they searched through tangles of laurel and honeysuckle, calling her name.

Forty more men from the CPS Camp joined the searchers on Tuesday. Still no luck. Wednesday morning, state police with bloodhounds, as well as hundreds of people from nearby towns, joined the search and were soaked by a late afternoon thunderstorm. But still no sign of little Doris Dean.

On Thursday, the searchers found her hair-clasp. More volunteers joined them and were terrified by the fury of a second thunderstorm that caught them high on the mountain. When Friday dawned, there seemed to be little hope for the barefoot child. By then, National Guard units, a Boy Scout troop, and horseback riders with dogs were scouring the trails. A low-flying airplane was aiding the search.

A final effort was planned for the weekend. A large group of volunteers met on Skyline Drive to search the hollows on both sides of the ridge. Three young men from the CPS Camp were assigned to follow the fire trail slightly to the south—today's Rocky Mount Trail. Henry Swartzenruber walked along the trail while Paul

Coffman and Luther Lurch scouted the area a hundred feet on either side. And in mid-afternoon, against all hope, near the peak of Rocky Mount, Paul found Doris! She was two or three miles from her home 1600 feet below. Her bare feet were blistered, and she was weak, thirsty, full of scratches and bruises, and covered with insect bites.

Paul stayed with the child while Henry and Luther "cut down through the mountainside through brush and undergrowth, sliding down cliffs on our hands and knees." They finally came to a logging road near the base of the mountain and "ran even faster than we had ever imagined possible" until they came to one of the search party's trucks. They were back at the child's home less than an hour from the time they found her.

Shots were fired and sirens blown to signal the rest of the volunteers that the search was over, and Henry and Paul led the rescue party back up the mountain. It took eight to ten men to carry Doris down over the cliffs on a makeshift stretcher. By the time they reached the logging road it was "lined for a mile with eager eyes trying to get a glimpse of the lost child." An ambulance was waiting to take her to the hospital.

None of the Park's later rescues attracted so many volunteers or involved the entire community the way this one did. The local radio station even broadcast bulletins to keep people informed about Doris's condition during the eleven days she was hospitalized with bronchial pneumonia after her ordeal.

As you hike the Rocky Mount Trail, imagine searchers combing the rugged slopes as gnats swarmed around their faces and hope faded that a small girl would be found alive.

Madison Run Road

Today's Madison Run Road follows the western leg of the old Browns Gap Turnpike, completed in 1806. When you hike here, you're walking on a historic road that carried many a peddler, wagon train, and soldier. This was the route used for years by Shenandoah Valley farmers taking produce across the mountains to Charlottesville as well as by Stonewall Jackson's army when it

The 1962 re-enactment of Stonewall Jackson's march through Browns Gap on what we now call the Madison Run Road.

marched eastward twice in 1862 (see p. 77).

You won't see any sign of this commercial and military activity on the Madison Run Road today, but you may find some remnants of the iron industry that flourished there in the second half of the nineteenth century.

Nearly 28,000 acres in this area were owned by the iron works that operated the Mount Vernon Furnace near the base of the road. Cooking pots, andirons, and other household items were cast here. But most of the iron was hauled five miles west to the the foundry in Port Republic. There it was cast into 300-pound "blooms." These blooms were loaded on barges and shipped down the South Fork of the Shenandoah to Harpers Ferry until the Civil War began. Then the iron was sent to Richmond and used for Confederate munitions.

When the trees are bare in winter, you can find the massive ruin of the Mount Vernon Furnace and stand inside its huge casting arch where molten iron once poured out. Nearby you'll see the long, rectangular pit that housed the waterwheel. Water diverted from Madison Run turned a huge overshot wheel that operated enormous bellows and forced air into the furnace.

The Mount Vernon Furnace (sometimes called the Margaret Jane Furnace) was actually a complex of buildings. It included an office, small dwellings for workers, and a shed that sheltered the massive masonry furnace. But the only structure that remains today is the crumbling furnace.* You can see its thick outer walls made of stone blocks about two feet high and four feet wide.

Noise filled the forest in the mid-nineteenth century: the clanging and clanking of picks and shovels as iron was mined from surface cuts a mile from the furnace, the ring of axes as trees were felled and hewed to supply the charcoal hearths, the clatter of ore cars on the narrow-gauge railway line leading to the furnace. (One piece of iron rail can still be found on the level area above the ruin.)

Activity in this now-peaceful place went on day and night. Once the furnace was fired, it operated around the clock for months. From the embankment behind the furnace, workers charged its blasting chamber with raw materials, emptying wagon-loads of ore, limestone, and charcoal into an opening at the base of the stack. (The limestone combined with impurities in the ore, forming a slag that floated to the top of the molten iron and was removed. The charcoal, besides fueling the furnace, produced carbon monoxide when its carbon combined with the oxygen in the blast of air from the bellows. This carbon monoxide, in turn, combined with the oxygen in the ore, leaving pure iron.)

On the ground below, other workmen opened the "cinder hole" at the back of the casting arch once each hour and raked out the accumulated slag. (You can still find hunks of slag in the area in front of the ruin.) And every twelve hours, the founder opened

---

*To reach the furnace site, follow the Madison Run Road west out of the Park to the locked gate at its base and continue along the state route for about 0.1 mile (passing two gravel roads branching off to the right) until you are opposite a house. You should be able to see the furnace ruin on the far side of the stream, inside the Park boundary. *Do not attempt to locate the ruin except during winter months or to cross the stream if the water is high. Remember, it is illegal to disturb the site or to remove anything from it.*

the tap hole in the casting arch and let the molten iron flow into trenches the gutterman had scraped in the deep sand in and beyond the casting arch. It was left to cool into molded iron bars, or "pigs"—so named because the arrangement of the trenches resembled a sow with a litter of nursing piglets around her.

While the furnace was in production, colliers, or charcoal makers, worked day and night at their hearths. Earlier, they had stacked two layers of three-foot logs on end, gradually sloping them inward around a central pole of green wood framed by pieces of saplings to form a small flue. When they finished, the mound was 30 or 40 feet in diameter.

Next they covered it with a layer of sticks until it resembled a dome. Last of all, they covered the pile with a thick layer of leaves and then four inches of charcoal dust or damp earth, filled the flue with kindling, shoveled in some hot coals, and sealed the opening.

During the days that followed, the colliers' job was twofold. They had to make sure the fire smoldering inside the mound didn't reach the surface. And they had to open vent holes near the ground on the leeward side of the mound so that gases wouldn't accumulate inside and cause it to explode.

Slowly, the logs were transformed to charcoal. Today, under layers of fallen leaves, large circles where the soil is covered with bits of carbon to a depth of several inches mark the places where the charcoal hearths smoldered.

Union forces destroyed the Mount Vernon Furnace in 1864, and it wasn't rebuilt for a decade. It was abandoned a few years later after the iron works property surrounding it was lost in a court case involving a land dispute. But the furnace could not have survived long in any event. Even before the war, Pennsylvania's furnaces had converted to cheaper anthracite coal instead of charcoal, the traditional fuel for iron furnaces. This doomed Virginia's iron industry. Virginia furnaces, with no hard coal supply, had difficulty competing. Without slave labor, competition became virtually impossible.

The silent remains of the Mount Vernon Furnace blending into the surrounding forest seem far removed from nineteenth-century industry. We find it hard to imagine today that the furnace's voracious appetite once denuded the surrounding land as the trees were cut for the charcoal hearths. (An acre of forest provided enough charcoal to fuel the furnace for just one day.) The passing years and protection as parkland have restored the forest here, and commerce, industry, and civil war are far from the minds of hikers on today's Madison Run Road.

The A.T. to Blackrock

From Browns Gap you can follow the Appalachian Trail south about 3.5 miles to Blackrock. Or you can make a one-mile round trip from the Blackrock area parking lot to the boulder-strewn viewpoint. This summit has long been a hikers' destination because of its panoramic vistas, and century-old initials are hidden beneath the dark lichens that give Blackrock its name.

But something of even greater interest was hidden here in the last quarter of the eighteenth century. During the Revolutionary War, when British Redcoats were threatening Virginia in the spring of 1781, the Virginia Assembly left the state capital for the relative safety of Charlottesville. Governor Thomas Jefferson gave the Virginia Archives and the state's Great Seal to his good friend, Bernis Brown, for safekeeping. Brown, whose family owned thousands of acres in the Blue Ridge, lived just east of Browns Gap. He kept the records at his home until the British drew so near he feared that the Commonwealth's treasures were again in danger.

Unwilling to risk the seal and documents, Brown, with the help of a local mountain man, loaded them onto mules. He led the mules up an old trail through Browns Gap to the top of the ridge and then south "up over the Black Rocks" where he hid the Archives in a cave. That cave cannot be found today. It may have been under a ledge that has since broken off, or it may simply have been a rocky crevice. But wherever it was, the records were safe.

The British pursuers caught up with some of the Assembly members in Charlottesville and captured them. Then they rode to Monticello. But Thomas Jefferson had been warned of their approach and escaped moments before they arrived. So the British got neither the author of the Declaration of Independence nor the "records of treason" that the King sought.

During the time those records were in Bernis Brown's care, many concerned Virginians asked where they were. Jefferson replied simply that they were safe. And safe they were, thanks to Brown's efforts. Brown's trip through the gap must have been a difficult one—this was a quarter century before his brother Brightberry and William Jarman built the turnpike. And there was no well-maintained Appalachian Trail leading from the gap to Blackrock until nearly a century and a half later. What a wilderness this patriot must have encountered in 1781!

The Black Rock Springs Hotel Site

Today we come to the Blue Ridge to be restored by its natural beauty, but earlier generations sought the restorative powers of the mineral springs that flowed from the depths of the mountains.

If you hike down the Paine Run Road, you will pass the site of the Black Rock Springs Hotel less than half a mile below Skyline Drive. (It will be on your right at the wide hairpin turn.) Advertisements claimed the waters at this nineteenth-century spa were "good for what ails you." One of its seven springs was said to cure gout, another to ease the pains of rheumatism, and still another to help cure baldness.

No one knows when the first hotel was built here, but it was mentioned as a resort in a Shenandoah Valley newspaper in 1835. Over the years, the people attracted to the mineral springs found varying accommodations.

Shortly before the Civil War, a New York company bought the hotel and renamed it Union Springs. Needless to say, this was not well received locally. A newspaper article about the resort listed "killing rattlesnakes" among the amusements offered.

Within two years, there was a new owner. Shortly thereafter, the war came, and he was forced to close the hotel. It reopened after the war, but times were hard and few people could afford to "take the waters" at Black Rock Springs. In 1873, creditors' demands forced the hotelkeeper to sell. His successor operated the resort for more than a decade, offering "dancing, card playing, croquet, tenpins, riding, and church picnics" as entertainment.

In the late 1880s, the Black Rock Springs Improvement Company was organized to promote and develop the area in much the same way that recreational land is developed today. Some of the local people bought lots and built summer cottages. These were made of wood frame and clapboard. Most had four rooms and a kitchen plus a wide front porch where the vacationers could chat or read.

Cottage owners tended to be older people who hoped to benefit from the mineral waters. But on weekends, buggies brought groups of young people from the Shenandoah Valley for picnics. The children and grandchildren of the cottage owners visited, too. Many of them climbed nearby Blackrock and scratched their initials on the boulders. Others enjoyed the bowling green or concerts at the bandstand.

It was a pleasant scene: two curving rows of well-kept cottages arranged around the three-story hotel with its wide veranda against a backdrop of mountain scenery. But trouble loomed ahead.

A gathering at Black Rock Springs, early in the 20th century.

Around the turn of the century, the Black Rock Springs Improvement Company faced financial difficulties. One problem was a suit by stockholders who claimed its officers had collected money for improvements that were never made—the situation with so many recreational developments today. Records show that the Company's holdings dropped from 1,400 acres to the 100 acres around the developed area.

A competitor then opened a boarding house and amusement building nearby. His establishment attracted a beer-drinking clientele not in keeping with the devout Brethren that owned many of the cottages. And as if that weren't enough, a dispute erupted between the Company and the newcomer about access to the water supply.

The Company built a fence between the spring and their rival, and some accounts say the owner of the boarding house diverted the water onto his property. Finally, the disagreement was settled in court. The ruling favored the Company, but not long after this, its officials sold the hotel and the acre of land surrounding it. The deed granted the new owner both a right-of-way for piping in the spring water and the privilege of using the recreational facilities.

The final event in this saga occurred in late autumn of 1909. A massive forest fire swept through the mountains and destroyed the Black Rock Springs Hotel and cottages. But the nearby boarding house somehow survived, and later it came to be known as the Black Rock Spring Hotel.

Paul Doug Harris, whose childhood home was on Browns Gap Road, remembered walking five or six miles to the Black Rock Springs Hotel with his brothers and sisters. They carried buckets of butter to sell at 10 cents a pound. He remembers Bob Miller's hotel and the three-lane bowling alley that attracted as many as 50 people on Saturday nights. Miller's hotel operated until the coming of the Park ended more than a century of commercial enterprise at Blackrock Springs.

The springs still flow, of course, and hikers sometimes explore the area. But there is little curiosity about the water once believed to have such wonderful powers that farmers bought it by the barrel to give to their sick animals.

* * *

Today, we see forests and wildflowers beside the trails where there were once fields and orchards. We see deer where cattle grazed and hogs foraged. We hear only birdsongs and rushing water where axes rang, where wagon trains clattered, where a furnace roared.

We meet other hikers where armies marched, where moonshiners lurked, where a president fished for trout. We see an occasional chimney or cabin ruin or graveyard but pass unaware scores of places where people lived and worked and laughed and wept. We will never know all of Shenandoah's secrets, but we know they are here.

Shenandoah National Park Archives

Authors' Note

The material in Shenandoah Secrets *is from many sources, published and unpublished. It was collected at public libraries and historical societies in the counties that surround the Park and at the Virginia State Library and Archives, the Virginia Historical Society, Alderman Library and Archives of the University of Virginia, the Potomac Appalachian Trail Club Archives, the Library of Congress, National Archives, and from the archives at Shenandoah National Park. Interviews with people who once lived in the area that became Park—or those who knew the mountain people—rounded out our never-ending search into formal sources with oral history.*

We are grateful to the many librarians and archivists who helped us; to the people who shared their memories with us; to Darwin Lambert, Paula Strain, and Len Wheat who critiqued the manuscript; and to Victoria Velsey, who helped proofread the galleys.

CR/JR
Glen Echo, Maryland
February 1991

167

Boots Dodson and his son.

Sources

Atkins, Sally. Author's interview, 1988.

Avery, Myron H. *In the Blue Ridge Mountains of Virginia.* Washington, D.C.: PATC, 1936.

Barbee family papers. Richmond: Virginia Historical Society.

Bates, David. *Breaking Trail in the Southern Appalachians—A Narrative.* Washington, D.C.: Potomac Appalachian Trail Club, 1987.

Beck, Ben. "Ten Days on the Appalachian Trail from Harper's Ferry to Skyland, 1935." Transcript of personal diary. Authors' files.

Beaty, Richard Edward. *The Blue Ridge Boys.* Front Royal: R. E. Beaty, 1938.

Benson, Harvey P. "The Skyline Drive, a Brief History of a Mountain Motorway." PATC *Bulletin* 9 (1940):67-71.

Berry, Gilbert. Authors' interviews, 1985.

Blue Ridge Copper Company, The. 1903. Pamphlet. Richmond: Virginia Historical Society.

Bolen, Beulah. Authors' interviews, 1978 and 1988.

Brown, Harold. Authors' interview, 1988.

Brown, Mozelle Cowden. Authors' interview, 1978.

Buck Family Papers. Front Royal: Warren Heritage Society.

Buck, George G. "A Sketch of Marcus Buck by His Grandson, George G. Buck." Typescript. 1940. Front Royal: Warren Heritage Society.

Cave, Elsie. Transcript of interview by Dorothy Noble Smith. Luray: SNP Archives.

Church, Randolph W. "Tidewater to Shenandoah Valley." *Virginia Cavalcade* 1 (1951):19-25.

Concise Illustrated History of the Civil War. Harrisburg: Historical Times: 1987.

Coleman, Elizabeth. "Virginia Buys a Hole in the Ground." *Virginia Cavalcade* 1 (1951):22-27.

Conway, Grant. "Range View: Second Walkie-Talkie with Frank Schairer." PATC *Bulletin* 32 (1963):9-10.

Cowan, John P. "The Range View Registers." PATC *Bulletin* 25 (1956):27.

Davis, M. G. *Madison County, Virginia: A Revised History.* Madison: County Board of Supervisors, 1977.

Dean, Gloria. *The Dean Mountain Story.* Washington, D.C.: Potomac Appalachian Trail Club, 1981.

169

Dockarty, Charles T. "Mountaineers Not Backward, Study Shows." *Washington Herald*, Jan. 11, 1932.

Eldred, Frances. Authors' interview, 1989.

Eppard, Irene and Roy. Authors' interviews, 1988.

Estes, Charles. Address at Rappahannock Historical Society meeting, Washington, Va., Jan. 8, 1988.

Floyd, Tom. *Lost Trails and Forgotten People: The Story of Jones Mountain.* Washington, D.C.: Potomac Appalachian Trail Club, 1981.

—————. "Trail Letter." *Potomac Appalachian* 18 (1989):3.

Fox, Merle. Authors' interviews, 1980, 1988.

Fry, Susan Winter. "The Civil War in Shenandoah National Park." Typescript. SNP: Big Meadows Library.

Fulkerson, Kathryn. "Twenty-five Years Ago." PATC *Bulletin* 23 (1954):103.

Gaines, William H., Jr. "Piedmont Bonanza." *Virginia Cavalcade* 16 (1967): 32-37.

Gaunt, Robert. "On the Trail of Andrew Gaunt: SNP Expedition." 1977. Typescript. Authors' files.

Glasser, Myron. "Explorations in the Southern Shenandoah National Park— 1930." PATC *Bulletin* 12 (1943):39-41.

Good, Leslie E. "Tanner and Delaney at Shenandoah Valley." *The Iron Man Album-Magazine*, July/Aug. 1983, pp. 1-4.

Greene County Record. Selected news articles, 1924-36.

Guide to Paths in the Blue Ridge. Washington, D.C.: PATC, 1931.

Hale, Laura Virginia. Selected papers. Warren Heritage Society.

Hampton, Joan. "The Primitive Life in Modern Virginia." *The Baltimore Sunday Sun*, May 1, 1932.

Hardesty's Historical and Geographical Encyclopedia. New York and Chicago: H. H. Hardesty & Co., 1884.

Harris, Paul Doug. Transcript of interview by Dorothy Noble Smith, 1977. Luray: SNP Archives.

Harrison Family Papers. Richmond: Virginia Historical Society.

Hawke, G. R. "Numerous Hotels and Taverns Hosted Early Visitors in Area." *Waynesboro News-Virginian*, July 17, 1979.

Heatwole, Henry. *Guide To Shenandoah National Park and Skyline Drive.* 4th rev. ed. Luray: Shenandoah Natural History Association, 1988.

Hite, Mary Elizabeth. *My Rappahannock Story Book.* Richmond: Dietz Press, 1950.

Hoak, Dale. Authors' interview, 1989.

Hoffman, Michael A. "A Synopsis of Patterns in Time: Human Adaptation in the Blue Ridge from 7000 B.C. to 1930 A.D." Report. 1979. Luray: SNP Archives.

Huth, Hans. "Report on Shenandoah National Park." Typescript. 1941. SNP: Big Meadows Library.

Horwitz, Elinor Lander. *Mountain People, Mountain Crafts.* Philadelphia and New York: Lippincott, 1974.

Jeffries, Margaret. *Virginia Folklore Collection.* Charlottesville: Alderman Library and Archives.

Johnson, Elizabeth B. and C.E., Jr. *Rappahannock County, Virginia: A History.* Orange, Virginia: Green Publishers, 1981.

Johnson, Elmer. Author's interview, 1988.

Lam, Howard. Transcript of interview by Dorothy Noble Smith, 1978. Luray: SNP Archives.

Lam, Zeda Haney. Authors' interviews, 1988.

Lambert, Darwin. *The Earth-Man Story.* Jericho: Exposition Press, 1972.

————. *Herbert Hoover's Hideaway.* Luray: Shenandoah Natural History Association, 1971.

————. "Shenandoah National Park Administrative History, 1924-1976." Report. NPS Mid-Atlantic Region and Shenandoah Natural History Association, 1979.

Land Ownership Files. Luray: SNP Map Archives.

Leich, Harold H. "Ski Tracks in the SNP." PATC *Bulletin* 18 (1949):2-6.

Life in Pocosan Hollow. Blue Ridge Mission Junior Club. Pamphlet. Richmond: Virginia State Library and Archives.

Madison County Eagle. Selected news articles, 1928-1936.

May, C. E. *My Augusta—A Spot of Earth, Not a Woman.* Bridgewater, Va.: Good Printers, 1987.

McCoy, Harold. Author's interview, 1989.

Miller, Minor R. "These Things I Remember." Typescript. SNP: Big Meadows Library.

Minor, James Fontaine. Correspondence, 1938-41. Charlottesville: Alderman Library and Archives.

Moody, Amanda. "Dark Hollow History." Typescript. SNP: Big Meadows Library.

————. "The Via Family." Typescript. SNP: Big Meadows Library.

Moon, William Arthur. *Historical Significance of Brown's Gap in the War Between the States.* 1937. Pamphlet. SNP: Big Meadows Library.

Moore, Samuel V. "The Crimora Manganese Mine." PATC Bulletin 16 (1947): 72-77.

Morris, Mary. Authors' interview, 1990.

Morris, Raymond E. Transcript of interview by Dorothy Noble Smith, 1969. Luray: SNP Archives.

Mountain Hospitality: Five Generations of Innkeeping at Graves Mountain Lodge. 1985. Pamphlet. Madison: Madison County Library.

Mountain Top Track, The. 1856. Pamphlet. Richmond: Virginia Historical Society.

"Mutiny Bared in CCC Camps." *Washington Times,* Nov. 18, 1937.

Ned's Tales of Rappahannock, compiled by Elizabeth B. Johnson, 1985. Pamphlet.

Neve, Archdeacon Frederick William. Collected Papers. Charlottesville: Alderman Library and Archives.

Newlon, Howard, Jr., and Nathaniel Mason Pawlett, et al, *Backsights.* Richmond: Virginia Department of Highways and Transportation, 1985.

Nicklin, Phillip Holbrook [Peregrine Prolix]. *Letters Descriptive of the Virginia Springs, the Roads Leading Therefrom and the Doings There in 1834 and 1835.*

Our Mountain Work in the Diocese of Virginia. Newsletter. Selected issues, 1911-1937.

Pawlett, Nathaniel Mason. "Historic Roads of Virginia." Charlottesville: Virginia Highway and Transportation Research Council, 1977.

———— and Howard Newlon, Jr. "Historic Roads of Virginia: The Route of the Three Notch'd Road—A Preliminary Report." Charlottesville: Virginia Highway and Transportation Research Council, 1976.

Perdue, Charles and Nancy. "Appalachian Fables and Facts." *Appalachian Journal*, Autumn/Winter 1979-80, pp. 84-104.

Peterson, Alvin E. "Some Nicholson Hollow Notes." PATC *Bulletin* 23 (1954):75.

Pollock, George Freeman. "Beginnings of Shenandoah National Park." PATC *Bulletin* 6 (1937):45-47.

————. *Skyland: The Heart of Shenandoah National Park.* Edited by Stuart E. Brown, Jr. Berryville: Chesapeake Book Co., 1960.

"Pre-Appalachian Trail Times—A Visit to the Blue Ridge in 1926." PATC *Bulletin* 12 (1943):18-24.

Protestant Episcopal Church in the USA, Virginia (Diocese) Papers, 1709-1972. Richmond: Virginia Historical Society.

Pullen, Lily. Author's interview, 1988.

Rappahannock Historical Society Vertical Files. Washington, Virginia.

Reeder, Carolyn and Jack. *Shenandoah Heritage: The Story of the People Before the Park.* Washington, D.C.: PATC, 1978.

Reeve, Sandy. Personal communication, 1990.

Schairer, Frank. "We Had Some Marvelous Times in the Old Days." PATC *Bulletin* 11 (1942):101-106.

Selmund, John A. *The Civilian Conservation Corps, 1933-1942: A New Deal Case Study.* Durham: Duke University Press, 1967.

Shoemaker, Michael. Personal correspondence, 1988.

Simmons, Dennis E. "Conservation, Cooperation, & Controversy: The Establishment of SNP, 1924-36." *Virginia Magazine of History and Biography* 89 (1981):387-404.

Spitler, Bernard, Jr. Authors' interview, 1988.

Stave and Barrel Machinery. Broadside. Richmond: Virginia State Historical Society.

Steere, Edward. "The Shenandoah National Park: Its Possibility as an Historic Development." Report. 1935. Luray: SNP Archives.

Stephens, W. T. "A Little Girl Is Lost." PATC *Bulletin* 12 (1944):31-35.

Stephenson, Jean. "From Browns Gap to Rockfish Gap." PATC *Bulletin* 5 (1936):94-96.

————. "Skyland Before 1900." PATC Bulletin 4 (1935):51-52.

Swartzentruber, Henry. *The Story of Doris Dean.* Pamphlet. Copy in authors' files.

Swindler, James E. Authors' interview, 1990.

Tarter, Brent. "All Men Are Equal Before Fishes." *Virginia Cavalcade* 15 (1981):156-165.

Tunis, Edwin. *Colonial Craftsmen and the Beginning of American Industry.* Cleveland and NY: The World Publishing Co., 1965.

Vandiver, Frank E. *Mighty Stonewall.* New York: McGraw Hill, 1957.

Wayland, John W. *Historic Homes in Northern Virginia.* Staunton: The McClure Co., 1937.

———. *Stonewall Jackson's Way.* Staunton: The McClure Co., 1940.

———. *Twenty-Five Chapters on the Shenandoah Valley.* Strasburg: Shenandoah Publishing House, 1957.

Williams, Elzie. Transcript of interview by Dorothy Noble Smith, 1977. SNP: Big Meadows Library.

Wood, Lola. Authors' interview, 1988, and personal correspondence.

Wood, Ray. Transcript of interview by Amanda Moody, 1977. Luray: SNP Archives.

Woods, Edgar. *Albemarle County in Virginia.* Bridgewater, Va.: Good Printers, 1930.

Woodward, Bessie Compton. Authors' interviews, 1978.

Young, Douglas. "A Brief History of the Staunton and James River Turnpike." Report. Richmond: Virginia Highway and Transportation Research Council, 1975.

Yowell, Claude Lindsay. *A History of Madison County, Virginia.* Strasburg: Shenandoah Publishing House, 1926.

Zerkel, Ferdinand. Collected papers. Luray: SNP Archives.

Zim, Herbert. "The Up and Down Sawmill and Adjacent Buildings." Report. 1944. SNP: Big Meadows Library.

The abandoned Old Rag School.

174

Index

Dark Hollow, 135-39; Church, 138, 140, 156; Falls, 140; School, 138, 140; Trail, 140

Dean: Doris, 157-58; James, 154; Luther, 64; men at sawmill, *155*; Stanton, 67-68

Dean Mountain, 67-69; cemetery, 154; School, 154

Depression, 79

Dickey Ridge, 38-39; Trail, 91

Distillery, 95, 151

Dodson, Jack, 107; Boots, with son, *184*

Dry Run Road, 154-156

Dundo Group Campground, 78

Dwyer: Francis Bolen, *93*

Early, Jubal, Gen., 58, 76

Eldred, Frances, 104

Engineer Training Placement Center, 142

Eppard, Irene Breeden, 154-56

Eviction: Cliser, *14*; on Tanners Ridge, 147-49

Fairfax Line, 62-63

Fairfax, Lord, 62

Fechner, Camp, 141

Fern Hill: 23; Church, *22*, 23, 67

Fishers Gap, 17, 58, 59, 62, 70, 136

Fire tower, 146

Fork Mountain, 146

Fox: Lemuel, 89-90; Merle, 14; Thomas, 89-90

Fox Farm 89-90

Fontaine, John, 17, 69

Fort Windham Rocks, 91

Franklin Cliffs, 58

Front Royal, 29, 32-33, 77, 91; entrance station, *32*

Gap, definition of, 3. *See also* names of individual gaps

Gaunt, Andrew, 98-99

Germanna, Va., 128

"Ghost forest," *61*, 136

Gliding, *61*

Gold, 107-108

Gordonsville Pike, 135-36, 138

Gravel (Gravelly) Spring, 41; Gap, 41

Graves: James Madison, 136; Mountain Lodge, 136; Paschal, 136

Gray: Jinney 98; Martha, 98; Oscar, 148

Grazing land, 57, 58, 71, 141
Gristmill, 4, 5, 6, 15, 19, 21, 123
Grottoes, Va., 29, 78
Guide to Paths in the Blue Ridge, 105

Haney: John, 20; Lula, 20, 22
Hannah Run Trail, 106, 108-110, 125
Harmony Hollow School, 90
Harris Hollow, 41; Trail, 41
Harris, Paul Doug, 165
Hawksbill: Gap, 30, 54-56; Mountain, 30, 44, 51, 54
Hawsburg (Hawburg, Hawberry), 8, 9, 10, 16, 104
Hazel: Church, 106; Country, 105-108; Hollow, 105-106; Mountain Trail,
          105-107; Road, Old, 105, 106; School, 106
Hensley: Church, 156; Hollow, 69; School, 156
Hessian soldiers, 84
Hightop, 69-70
Hill, A.P., General, 62
Hollow Folk, 125
Honeymoon Cottage, *146*
Hoover: Camp, 29, 31, 59, 142-47; Camp map, *143*; School, *144*, 145
Hoover, Herbert, 29, 62, 138, 142
Hoskins, Taylor, 53
Hughes River: Church, 125; School, 125
Hull School, 96, 101, *102*; Trail, 42, 101, 103
Hut (shelter). *See* Byrd's Nest; Indian Run; Old Rag; Pass Mountain
Hutchins Ordinary, 7

Indian Run, 91
Iron industry. *See* Mount Vernon Furnace; Germanna, Va.

Jackson, "Stonewall", Gen., 18, 33, 37, 58, 62, 69, 76, 77, 136, 158; march
          re-enactment, *159*
Jarman Gap, 84-86
Jarman, Thomas, 84; William, 76
Jefferson, Thomas, 162-63
Jenkins: Ashby, 135; Nathan, 107-108
Jinney Gray Road, 98
Johnson, Ned, 108
Jones Mountain: Cabin, 150; Trail, 150-51

Kelly, Dr. J.T., 99-100

Pomeroy, Alex, 91-92
Possoms Rest, 91-92
Potomac Appalachian Trail Club (PATC), 39-40, 45, 73, 112, 150, 152, 167
Price Lands, 47
Prohibition, 106, 123, 126, 151

Rapidan Road, 143
Range View Cabin, 99-101
Rattlesnake Point, 99
Reconstruction, 64
Red Gate Road, 58
Revolutionary War, 10, 84, 162
Rock Spring Cabin, 58
Rockfish Gap, 3, 25-26; entrance, 25; Turnpike, 85
Rocky Mount Trail, 157-58
Rolling road, 18, 26, 105
Roosevelt, Franklin D., 31, 47, 60
Rose River: Loop, 135; Road, 135-36; Trail, 140

Saddle Trail, 135
Sam's Ridge Trail, 106
Sawmill, 4, 5, 6, 15, 19, 65, 67, 151, 90, 91, 151, 155, 156
Schools: Beahm, 12; Church of the Brethren Industrial, 23, 68; Dark Hollow, 140; Dean Mountain, 154; Fern Hill, 22, 23;; Harmony Hollow, 90; Hazel Hollow, 106; Hoover, 106; Lost Mountain, 75; Maple Springs, 156; Nicholson Hollow, 51, 125; Old Rag, 131-32; Pocosin, 153; Simmons Gap, 70-74; Simpson's private, 33; Sperryville High, 96; Sunnyside, 21; Tanners Ridge, 147
Sexton: Cabin, 45-46; Knoll Picnic Area, 46, 47
Sexton, Roy L., 45, 50, 52
Sheridan, Gen. Phillip, 76
Sheep, 16, 99
Shenandoah Valley, 4, 18, 58, 59, 84, 85, 136, 140, 147, 158, 163, 164; Campaign, 33, 77
Shipp Tavern, 24
Simmons Gap, 71-74, 75; Mission, 72, 73; School, 70, 72; Store and Post Office, 73
Simpson: Mary, 33; Place, 33-34; Samuel Jefferson, 33
Sisk, Charlie, 99-100
Ski area, 45
Skinner, Frank, 8
Skyland, 29, 45, 48-52, 53, 113, 121, 122, 125, 141, 146
Skyland, 125